Original Badisch
The Best of Baden Food

HÄDECKE

Monika Graff · Heidi Knoblich

Original Badisch
The Best
of Baden Food

Abkürzungen

kg – Kilogramm
g – Gramm
l – Liter
ml – Milliliter
EL – Esslöffel
TL – Teelöffel

Abbreviations

c(s). – cup(s)
lbs(s). – pound(s)
oz(s). – ounce(s)
qt. – quart (2 pints)
tbsp. – tablespoon
tsp. – teaspoon

© Walter Hädecke Verlag, Weil der Stadt, 2003
2. Auflage 2007
www.haedecke-verlag.de

Abbildung Vor- und Nachsatz aus EMAIL von Brigitte ten Kate von Eicken (Archiv Hädecke)

Foodstyling: Andreas Miessmer, Lahr
Fotografie: Fritz Frech, Offenburg
Umschlaggestaltung:
nett & artig, Julia Graff, Düsseldorf
Typografie und Satz: ES Typo-Graphic,
Ellen Steglich, Stuttgart
Reproduktionen: Raff digital, Riederich

ISBN 978-3-7750-0416-9

Picture endlives from
EMAIL by Brigitte ten Kate von Eicken

Foodstyling: Andreas Miessmer, Lahr
Photos: Fritz Frech, Offenburg
Cover design:
nett & artig, Julia Graff, Düsseldorf
Typography and typesetting:
ES Typo-Graphic, Ellen Steglich, Stuttgart
Reproductions: Raff digital, Riederich

Printed in EU, 2007

Ne freudig Stündli,
isch's nit e Fündli?
Jetz hemmer's und jetz simmer do.

JOHANN PETER HEBEL

Rezepte

Recipes

Baden als solches gibt es nicht mehr. Es lebt nur noch in den Herzen nostalgischer Träumer und den Hildabrötchen, die an die letzte Großherzogin erinnern. Aber die badischen Landschaften und die Badener selber existieren noch. Sie haben auch die nachkriegsbedingte Vernunftehe der äußerst widerspenstigen badischen Braut mit Württemberg unbeschadet überlebt, bei der die Liebe erst nach der Heirat kam, aber schon allein wegen des Spätzleteigs in Gefahr ist; die Badenerin nimmt an Stelle des Wassers lieber ein Ei mehr.

Doch Baden ist mehr als ein geographischer Begriff, der vom behäbigen Bodensee über das Dreiländereck bis hinunter über Baden-Baden und Heidelberg nach Mannheim ins Bauland, der Heimat des Dinkels, reicht. Baden. Schon allein der Klang seines Namens verheißt Wärme, Wasser, Sommervergnügen, Eleganz, Bodenständiges, Weltgewandtes – Lebenslust pur. So richtig badisch, weltoffen, selbstbewusst und gelassen gibt man sich allerdings nur im „Altbadischen", bei den Markgräflern, Kaiserstühlern und Freiämtlern, da, wo man eben schon immer badisch und evangelisch war. Da, wo man den offenen Blick gegen Westen hat, von wo der Freiheitsgedanke herüberwehte.

Dieses Baden, das mit Hilfe der Französischen Revolution geboren wurde, würfelte durch napoleonische Flurbereinigung katholische und reformierte und kirchliche und weltliche Gebiete zu einem regelrechten Menschenkaleidoskop zusammen. Zu der wiedervereinigten Markgrafschaft gesellte sich nämlich 1806 noch die Provinz Vorderösterreich, deren Relikt die älteste Torte der Welt, die Linzer Torte, zum Nationalheiligtum Badens geworden ist. Diese katholische Provinz bestand einst aus dem Breisgau, der Ortenau und den Waldstädten am Hochrhein und Teilen des Elsass

Bei den Schwarzwäldern und den Hotzenwäldern ist es daher nicht so weit her mit diesem badischen Gefühl. Sie wirken nach außen hin eher verschlossen, grüblerisch und trauen

nur dem lieben Gott und sich selbst. Sie lehnen seit jeher jeden Zwang ab und suchen nach Freiheit und Unabhängigkeit, was sie im 18. Jh. im Hotzenwald zu Sozialrevolutionären, den Salpeterern, werden ließ, die sich gegen Staat und Kirche erhoben. Nirgendwo wurde die 1848er Revolution so heftig und auf so breiter Ebene getragen wie in Baden.

Baden hat viele Gesichter. Das der blühenden Kirschbäume im Eggener Tal im Markgräfler Land und der tosenden, schroff vom Feldberg herabstürzenden Menzenschwander Alb. Das der wohlgeordneten Weinberge den Oberrhein entlang bis in die Ortenau, der flirrenden Hitze auf dem Isteiner Klotzen und im Kaiserstuhl, das der tobenden Schneestürme auf dem Feldberg und die Barocktürme der Klöster St. Märgen und St. Peter. Baden, das ist das Röttler Schloss, die Hofsgrunder Käsle, der Belchen, der Hausberg des Markgräfler Landes, der wie ein Elefantenbuckel hoch über dem Münstertal und der Rheinebene thront. Baden ist da, wo Europa längst Alltag ist, wo man Verwandte hat über den Rhein und die gemeinsame alemannische Sprache verbindet.

Baden hatte im Markgrafen Karl Friedrich, der 1804 zum Großherzog dieses neuen Landes wurde, den edelsten und aufgeklärtesten deutschen Fürsten, der zudem noch den „Markgräfler", den Gutedel erfunden hat. Es hatte die erste deutsche Majolikamanufaktur und Hans Thoma, den Fürstenmaler Franz Xaver Winterhalter, den bis heute ungeklärten Hofskandal und Kriminalfall Kaspar Hauser, seinen Simplicissimus, den Trompeter von Säckingen, und es hatte Johann Peter Hebel, der am Karlsruher Hof die alemannische Sprache salonfähig machte.

Badens Herz schlägt auf dem Freiburger Münsterplatz, der von Gasthäusern umgeben ist und auf dem beim Wochenmarkt der bunte Markgräfler Garten ausgebreitet liegt und alle Sinne betört.

Baden lives on only in the hearts of nostalgic dreamers and in the Hilda cookies which remind us of the last Grand Duchess. But the inhabitants of Baden still exist. They have even survived, intact, the post-war marriage of convenience between the extremely recalcitrant Baden bride and Württemberg, a marriage in which love only blossomed after the wedding, but one which is still endangered even by the composition of the batter for Spätzle: Baden housewives prefer an extra egg instead of water.

But Baden is more than a geographical concept stretching from leisurely Lake Constance via the point where Germany, Switzerland and France meet, right down the Rhine via Baden-Baden and Heidelberg to Mannheim and the Bauland. Baden. Even the sound of its name conjures up warmth, water, summer pleasures, elegance, local patterns of living and international sophistication – pure "lebenslust". Yet the real Baden temperament – openness to the world and equanimity – will only be found in "Old Baden", among the inhabitants of the Markgräfler, Kaiserstuhl and Freiämt regions, where the people have always been Badeners and evangelical.

This Baden was moulded into a veritable human kaleidoscope via the Napoleonic land reform, which rolled Catholic and Reformed regions, ecclesiastical and secular areas into one big ball. In 1806, the Evangelical margraviate was extended by the Catholic province of Outer Austria, with Breisgau, Ortenau and the Forest Towns as well as parts of Alsace. This fusion brought with it the oldest gâteau in the world: Linz Gâteau, the treasured national possession of Baden, with which "Markgräfler" wine is drunk here.

So the inhabitants of the Black Forest and the Hotzenwald do not share this Baden outlook to the same extent. They resist any compulsion and search for freedom and independence, a trait which, in Hotzenwald in the 18th century, turned them into social revolutionaries named "Saltpeterers", who rebelled against both State and Church. Nowhere was the 1848 revolution pursued as violently and on so broad a front as in Baden.

Baden has many faces. Cherry trees in bloom in the Eggener Valley in the Markgräfler Land and the windswept Menzenschwander Alb that rolls steeply down from the Feldberg. The neatly planted vineyards along the Upper Rhine as far as the Ortenau region, the shimmering heat on the Isteiner Klotzen and in the Kaiserstuhl area, the raging snowstorms on the Feldberg and the baroque towers of the monasteries of St. Märgen and St. Peter. Baden is cheerful Lake Constance, the Hofsgrunder Käsle, the Belchen, which towers above the Rhine levels like an elephant's back. Baden is where Europe has long been a part of everyday life, where the people have relatives on the other side of the Rhine.

Margrave Karl Friedrich, the inventor of the "Gutedel" grape, who became Grand Duke of this new country in 1804, was the noblest and most enlightened German ruler. Baden had Germany's first majolica manufactory and Hans Thoma, the painter of princes Franz Xaver Winterhalter, the court scandal and criminal case of Kaspar Hauser. It had the magazine Simplicissimus, the "Trumpeter of Säckingen", and Johann Peter Hebel, who made the Alemannic dialect acceptable at the court in Karlsruhe.

Baden's heart beats on Freiburg's Münsterplatz, where the daily market spreads out the colourful Markgräfler and Kaiserstuhl produce to dazzle all our senses. Franzeli was once at home here, a heavyweight character, a real Baron of Neuveu and gourmet. As a young boy he was looking for a present for his mother. He wanted a globe, but he didn't have enough money for the one in the stationer's shop on Münsterplatz. He told the lady shopkeeper that he was thinking of something smaller, a little globe just of Baden, perhaps.

Kartoffelsupp' mit Holderküchle

Potato soup with "Holderküchle"

Kartoffelsupp' mit Holderküchle

1 kg mehlig kochende Kartoffeln
1 Zwiebel, gehackt
1 Gelbe Rübe, gehackt
das Weiße von 1 Stange Lauch oder ein Stück
   Sellerie, gehackt
30 g Butter
1,5 l gut gewürzte Fleischbrühe
$1/_8$ l süße Sahne (Rahm)
Salz und Pfeffer, frisch gemahlen

Die Kartoffeln schälen und in Blättchen schneiden. Die gehackten Gemüse in der zerlassenen Butter anschwitzen, Kartoffelscheiben zugeben und kurz mit andämpfen. Mit einem Liter Brühe auffüllen und alles weich kochen. Durch ein Sieb oder mit der Flotten Lotte passieren.
Mit der restlichen Brühe auffüllen, erhitzen, mit Sahne abrunden und nachwürzen.

Anmerkung: Die Suppe kann noch mit fein gehackten und in wenig Butter angeschwitzten Gemüsewürfeln oder mit Kracherle, siehe Seite 24, bestreut werden.

Holderküchle – Holderchüechli

Ausbackteig:
125 g Mehl, 2 Eier, getrennt
1–2 Esslöffel Zucker, 1 Prise Salz
knapp $1/_4$ l helles Bier
oder Milch und ein Schuss Bier
12–16 frisch gepflückte Holunderdolden*
Butterschmalz zum Ausbacken
Puderzucker zum Bestäuben

Aus Mehl, Eigelb, Zucker, Salz und Bier einen dünnflüssigen Teig rühren und 20 bis 30 Minuten quellen lassen. Dann das steif geschlagene Eiweiß vorsichtig unterheben.
Die Blütendolden gut ausschütteln – möglichst nicht waschen –, jeweils einzeln in den Teig tauchen und im erhitzten Butterschmalz in etwa 2 Minuten goldgelb ausbacken, auf Küchenkrepp abtropfen lassen und mit Puderzucker bestreut lauwarm servieren.

Der Holunderbaum wird in alten Mythen mit Frau Holle in Verbindung gebracht, und der Bauer zog früher aus Verehrung vor ihm den Hut. Er gilt seit jeher als „Medizinschrank Gottes". Seine heilenden Wirkstoffe stecken in den Wurzeln, Blättern, Blüten und Beeren. Zum Schutz vor bösen Geistern und Blitzschlag pflanzte man ihn als Hausbaum, und es war bei Strafe verboten, ihn zu fällen.
Er gehörte früher zu jedem Bauernhof. Im Frühjahr wurden die Blüten für Holderküchle oder Sekt verwendet; die fast schwarzen Beeren ergaben im Herbst köstliches Gelee, Likör und Sirup, der im Winter heiß genossen gegen Fieber und Grippe half. Heute genießt man in der gehobenen Gastronomie klaren Holundersirup, aufgegossen mit Winzersekt als besonderen Aperitif.

---

* Neben Holunderblüten eignen sich auch Akazienblüten sowie Zitronenmelisse- und Salbeiblättchen („Salbeimäusle") zum Ausbacken.

Potato soup

2 lbs. 3 ozs. potatoes boiled until they are mealy
1 onion, chopped
1 carrot, chopped
the white part of 1 leek or a piece of celeriac, chopped
1 oz. butter
1.5 US qt. (3½ GB pints) well seasoned meat stock
¼ c. fresh cream
salt and pepper, freshly ground

Peel the potatoes and slice them into leaves. Simmer the chopped vegetables in melted butter until soft but not brown, add the potato slices and continue to simmer for a short time. Top up with one quart of stock and boil until all ingredients are soft. Pass through a sieve or a "Flotte Lotte" (German hand-operated rotary purée-maker). Add the rest of the stock, heat up, round off with the cream and season to taste.

Note: This soup can be sprinkled with finely chopped vegetable cubes gently and briefly fried in a little butter or with "Kracherle", see page 25.

"Holderküchle" (elderblossom fritters)

Batter for frying:
4 ozs. flour, 2 eggs, separated
1–2 tbsp. of sugar, 1 pinch of salt
just under ½ c. light ale
or milk with a dash of beer
12–16 freshly picked elderberry blossoms*
clarified butter or ghee for frittering
icing sugar to dredge

Mix a thin batter from the flour, egg yolks, sugar, salt and beer and allow to thicken for 20 to 30 minutes. Then carefully fold in the stiffly beaten egg whites.
Shake the elder blossoms well – do not wash them, if possible – and dip them individually in the batter. Fritter them in the hot clarified butter for about 2 minutes until they are golden yellow in colour, place on sheets of kitchen roll to allow the fat to drip off and serve lukewarm and dredged with icing sugar.

In old myths, the elder tree ("Holunderbaum") was associated with Frau Holle (the spirit who watched over domesticity and household morals), and farmers used to doff their caps out of respect when they passed one. The tree has always been part of "God's Medicine Chest". Its healing powers are in the roots, leaves, blossoms and berries. It was planted next to the house as protection against evil spirits and lightning strikes, and it was a punishable offence to fell one. In spring the blossoms were used for "Holderküchle" or sparkling wine ("Sekt"); in autumn the black berries were turned into a delicious jelly, liqueur or syrup which, drunk hot in winter, alleviated fevers and influenza. Today, clear elderberry syrup topped up with vintner's "sekt", is enjoyed as an exclusive aperitif in superior gastronomic circles.

---

* In addition to elderberry blossoms, acacia blossoms as well as lemon-balm or sage leaves ("Sage mice") are suitable for dipping in this batter.

Schneckensüpple · Snail soup

Schneckensüpple

Gemüse:

1 Gelbe Rübe, 1 Zwiebel
1 Stange Lauch, 1 Petersilienwurzel
100 g weiße frische Champignons
$1/2$ l Fleischbrühe oder Kalbsbrühe
$1/2$ l trockener Weißwein
1 Lorbeerblatt
20 g Butter
1 Dose Schnecken (24 Stück)
2 Schalotten
2–3 Knoblauchzehen, fein gehackt

Zum Binden:

2 Eigelb
$1/8$ l süße Sahne oder Crème double
Salz und weißer Pfeffer, frisch gemahlen
2 Esslöffel Petersilie, fein gehackt

Alle Gemüse waschen, putzen, zerkleinern und in der Butter anschwitzen. Mit Brühe und Wein auffüllen, das Lorbeerblatt einlegen und die Suppe bei geringer Hitzezufuhr ca. 30 Minuten köcheln.
Die Schnecken aus der Dose nehmen – die Flüssigkeit aufbewahren – und in feine Streifen schneiden oder einen Teil halbieren und den Rest hacken.
Zusammen mit den gehackten Schalotten und Knoblauchzehen in Butter andünsten. Den Schneckensaft sowie die durchgesiebte Gemüsebrühe zugießen und alles in etwa 5 Minuten erhitzen. Eigelb mit Sahne oder Crème double verquirlen und die Suppe damit legieren. Mit Salz und Pfeffer abschmecken und mit gehackter Petersilie bestreuen.

Anmerkung: Die Schneckensuppe ist ein einfaches, bäuerliches Essen, von dem es viele unterschiedliche Rezepte gibt. Oft wird zur Bindung verquirlte Kartoffelstärke verwendet. Geschmacklich kann die Suppe noch mit frisch geriebener Muskatnuss abgerundet werden.

Saures Topinambur-Gemüse

360 g Topinamburknollen (Erdartischocken)

Sauce:

50 g Butter oder halb Butter, halb Pflanzenöl
1 kleine Zwiebel – weiß oder rot –, gehackt
Salz und Pfeffer, frisch gemahlen
1 Esslöffel Weißweinessig
1 Bund Schnittlauch, fein geschnitten

Topinamburknollen abbürsten und ungeschält in Salzwasser weich kochen, mit kaltem Wasser abschrecken. Schälen und in Würfel oder Scheiben schneiden. Butter oder Butter und Pflanzenöl erhitzen, die Zwiebel darin anschwitzen, mit Salz, Pfeffer und Essig würzen. Topinambur einlegen, vermischen, mit Schnittlauch bestreut servieren.

Anmerkung: Topinambur ist ein Knollengewächs, das ursprünglich von den Indianern Nordamerikas angebaut wurde. Im Badischen wird daraus auch ein beliebter Schnaps gebrannt.

Bodenkohlraben-Gemüse

1,5 kg Bodenkohlraben (Steckrüben), geschält und in etwa 3 cm große Würfel geschnitten
Salzwasser
2 Esslöffel Schmalz oder anderes Fett
1–2 Esslöffel feiner Zucker oder Puderzucker
1 Zwiebel, fein gehackt
Salz und Pfeffer, frisch gemahlen

Die Rübenwürfel in Salzwasser knackig garen. Abgießen und abtropfen lassen.
Fett in einer großen Pfanne zerlassen, den Zucker darin karamellisieren lassen, die Zwiebeln hell anschwitzen und die Rüben zugeben. Evtl. etwas Wasser angießen und die Rüben ca. 15 Minuten dämpfen.
Dazu passen Salzkartoffeln, grüner, gekochter Bauchspeck oder Hammelfleisch.

Snail soup

Vegetables etc.:
   1 carrot
   1 onion
   1 leek
   1 parsley root
3 1/2 ozs. fresh white mushrooms
   1 c. meat stock or veal stock
   1 c. dry white wine
   1 bay leaf
2/3 oz. butter
   1 tin of snails (contents: 24)
   2 shallots
2–3 cloves of garlic, finely chopped

To thicken:
   2 egg yolks
1/4 c. single or double cream
salt and white pepper, freshly ground
   2 tbsp. of finely chopped parsley

Wash, clean and prepare all the vegetables before simmering them in the butter until soft but not brown. Add the stock and the wine, add the bay leaf and simmer the soup for approx. 30 minutes. Take the snails out of the tin – keep the liquid – and cut them in thin slices or cut half of the amount into half and chop the other ones.
Fry them together with the chopped shallots and garlic in butter. Add liquid and stock and bring to the boil, simmering for about 5 minutes.
Beat the egg yolks with the cream or crème double and dredge the soup with the mixture. Season with salt and pepper and sprinkle with chopped parsley.

Note: This snail soup is a simple, rustic dish and there are lots of similar recipes. It is quite common to use potato starch for thickening. To provide a finer flavour you can season this soup with freshly ground nutmeg.

Sour Jerusalem artichokes

13 ozs. Jerusalem artichokes

For the sauce:
1 3/4 ozs. butter or half butter, half vegetable oil
   1 small onion – white or red -, chopped
salt and pepper, freshly ground
   1 tbsp. white wine vinegar
   1 bunch of chives, finely chopped

Clean the artichokes by brushing and boil them in their skins in seasoned water until tender, rinse them in cold water. Peel them and dice or slice into strips. Heat the butter or butter and vegetable oil and fry the onions until soft but not brown, adding a seasoning of salt, pepper and vinegar. Add the artichokes, mix together and sprinkle with chopped chives before serving.

Note: The Jerusalem artichoke is a plant originally cultivated by the North American Indians. In Baden, a popular schnapps is also distilled from its cream-coloured tubers.

Swede cubes

3 lbs. 3 ozs. swedes, peeled and cut into cubes
   of about 1 inch
salted water
   2 tbsp. lard or other fat
1–3 tbsp. caster sugar or icing sugar
   1 onion, finely chopped
salt and pepper, freshly ground

Boil the swede cubes in salted water until they are crunchy. Strain and allow the drops to drain off. Melt the fat in a large pan, brown the sugar in it, fry the onions until they are soft but not brown and add the swede cubes. Add a little water if necessary and steam for approx. 15 minutes. This dish goes well with boiled potatoes, boiled unsalted streaky bacon or mutton.

*Löwenzahnsalat
mit Speck und Kracherle*

*Dandelion salad
with bacon and "Kracherle"*

Löwenzahnsalat mit Speck und Kracherle

200g frische Löwenzahnblätter
  4 Scheiben durchwachsener Speck
  1 Scheibe Bauernbrot oder
  2 Scheiben Weißbrot
10 g Butter

Vinaigrette:
Salz und Pfeffer, frisch gemahlen
  1 Teelöffel mittelscharfer Senf
  1 Esslöffel Rotweinessig
2–3 Esslöffel Raps- oder Walnussöl

Die Löwenzahnblättchen waschen, gut abtropfen lassen und größere Blätter halbieren; auf vier Tellern auslegen.
Die Speckscheiben ohne Fett in einer Pfanne kross braten, auf Küchenkrepp abtropfen lassen, dann in Streifen brechen oder zu Stückchen bröseln. Brotscheiben würfeln und in der Butter leicht anbräunen. Die Vinaigrette anrühren, über den Löwenzahnblättern verteilen, mit Speck und Brotwürfeln bestreuen.

Anmerkung: Im benachbarten Elsass heißt dieser Salat: Salade au pissenlit. Das Wort „pissenlit" heißt in der Übersetzung „Bettseicher" – und so wird der Löwenzahn auch in der Mundart genannt., weil er harntreibende Wirkung hat.

Und „Kracherle"? Die angerösteten Brotwürfel krachen zwischen den Zähnen wenn man darauf beißt.

Nüsslisalat

200 g Acker-, Feld- oder Nüsslisalat*

Vinaigrette:
  1 Schalotte, sehr fein gehackt
nach Belieben: 1 Knoblauchzehe, durchgepresst
Salz und Pfeffer, frisch gemahlen
  1 Teelöffel körniger Senf
  1 Esslöffel Weißweinessig
  1 Prise Zucker
2–3 Esslöffel Kürbiskern- oder Walnussöl

Die kleinen Würzelchen von den Salat-Rosetten abschneiden, aber die Salatpflanzen möglichst ganz lassen. Den Salat gründlich waschen, gut abtropfen lassen oder in der Salatschleuder trocknen. Auf Teller oder in Salatschüsselchen verteilen.
Die Vinaigrette anrühren, über den Nüsslisalat träufeln. Oder die Vinaigrette in einer Salatschüssel anrühren, die Rosetten hineingeben und gut mit der Sauce vermischen. Sofort auf Teller verteilen und servieren.
Der Salat kann wie der Löwenzahnsalat auch mit Speck und Kracherle, Rezept nebenstehend, gereicht werden.

---

* In Südbaden nennt man den Nüsslisalat liebevoll „Sunnewirbeli" (Sonnenwirbel).

Dandelion salad with bacon and "Kracherle"

7 ozs. fresh dandelion leaves
4 slices streaky bacon
1 slice rustic bread or
2 slices white bread
1 tbsp. butter

Dressing:
salt and pepper, freshly ground
1 tsp. mustard, medium hot
1 tbsp. red-wine vinegar
2–3 tbsp. rape oil or walnut oil

Wash the dandelion leaves, thoroughly drain the water off and cut bigger leaves into half; spread them on four plates. Fry the bacon in a frying pan without any oil until crunchy, allow the grease to trickle off on a piece of kitchen towel, then break the bacon into strips or crumble into pieces. Dice the slices of bread and fry them lightly in butter until brown. Blend the dressing, spread over the dandelion leaves, and sprinkle with bacon and bread cubes.

Note: In the neighbouring region of Alsace, this salad is called: Salade au pissenlit. The word "pissenlit" translates as "pee-bed" – and dandelion is called "Bettseicher" (= "pee-bed") in the local dialect because of its diuretic properties.

And "Kracherle"? The diced and roasted bread crackles between the teeth when chewed.

"Nüsslisalat" lamb's-lettuce salad

7 ozs. lamb's lettuce, corn-salad or
"Nüsslisalat"*

Dressing:
1 shallot, very finely chopped
if desired: 1 clove of garlic, mashed
salt and pepper, freshly ground
1 tsp. grainy mustard
1 tbsp. white-wine vinegar
1 pinch of sugar
2–3 tbsp. pumpkin-seed oil or walnut oil

Cut off the small roots from the bunches of leaves, leaving the plants unseparated wherever possible. Rinse the leaves thoroughly, pat dry or swing dry in a salad basket. Place the salad on plates or in small bowls. Mix the ingredients of the dressing together and sprinkle over the salad or stir up the dressing in a salad bowl, add the salad rosettes and mix everything together with the cream. Put on plates immediately and serve. Like dandelion salad, this salad can be served with bacon or "Kracherle", see previous recipe.

---

* In the south of Baden, "Nüsslisalat" is charmingly called "Sunnewirbeli" (sun whorls).

Spargel und Schinken

Kratzede

2 kg weißer Spargel, möglichst frisch
gestochen
1/2 l Gemüsebrühe
20 g Butter
1 Prise Salz
1 Teelöffel Zucker
1 Teelöffel Zitronensaft

Zum Anrichten:
2 hart gekochte Eier, gehackt

Pro Person
50 g gekochter und
50 g roher Schinken, z. B. Schwarzwälder
Schinken
evtl. 60 g Butter zum Übergießen

Spargel waschen, die Enden, die evtl. holzig sein
können, abschneiden und die Spargelstangen
vom Kopf her mit dem Spargelschäler abschälen.
Anschließend die Spargel evtl. auf gleiche Länge
kürzen und mit Küchengarn zu vier Bündeln zu-
sammenbinden.
In einem hohen Spargelkochtopf die Spargelschalen mit der Gemüsebrühe, der Butter, Salz,
Zucker und Zitronensaft ca. 10 Minuten kochen.
Die Spargelschalen entfernen und die Spargelstangen in den Einsatz stellen und im sanft ko-
chenden Spargelsud ca. 15–20 Minuten garziehen lassen (Die Garzeit richtet sich nach der
Frische des Spargels).

Anrichten: Jeweils eine Portion (Faden entfernen)
Spargel auf vorgewärmten Tellern mit gehacktem
Ei bestreuen, Kratzede sowie Schinkenscheiben
dazu legen. Wer möchte, kann noch Butter zer-
lassen und diese über die Spargel gießen.
Kleine, ausgestochene, in Butter geschwenkte
Kartoffeln oder dünne Pfannkuchen (siehe Abb.)
passen auch gut dazu.

4 Eier
250 g Weizenmehl
ca. 1/8 l Milch und etwas Mineralwasser
1 Prise Salz.
2–3 Esslöffel Butterschmalz oder Sonnenblumenöl oder Rapsöl

Für süße Kratzete:
1 Esslöffel Zucker
Puderzucker

Eier mit Mehl gut verrühren, am besten mit der
Küchenmaschine oder dem Handrührer, sodass
keine Klümpchen bleiben. Langsam Flüssigkeit
einlaufen lassen, salzen, evtl. zuckern und alles
gut verrühren – der Teig soll nicht dünnflüssig
sein. Mindestens 30 Minuten stehen lassen, damit
der Teig ausquellen kann.
Teig nach dem Ruhen noch einmal durchrühren.
In einer Eisenpfanne oder in einer beschichteten
Pfanne etwas Fett erhitzen, die Pfanne damit aus-
schwenken und so viel Teig einfüllen, dass der Boden davon bedeckt ist. Den Pfannkuchen so lange
anbacken, bis die Masse beginnt auf der Oberfläche zu stocken, dann wenden, kurz anbacken
und sofort mit Hilfe einer Backschaufel in kleine
Stücke trennen und fertig backen.
Fertige Kratzete warm halten und alles zum
Schluss noch einmal in der Pfanne vermischen.

Anmerkung: Süße Kratzete wird mit Puderzucker
bestäubt zum Nachtisch mit Kompott serviert.

Woher kommt der Name „Kratzete" – Chratzede,
auch Kratzet, Durnand und auch Dummiss genannt . – Beim Trennen des Pfannkuchens in kleine Stücke macht die Backschaufel ein kratzendes
Geräusch! – Dieses Gericht ist eng verwandt mit
dem österreichischen „Schmarrn" – was nicht
verwunderlich ist, da der Breisgau, die Ortenau
und der Schwarzwald mit den Waldstädten am
Hochrhein einst zu „Vorderösterreich" gehörten.

Asparagus and ham

4½ lbs. white asparagus, if possible freshly
    cut
1 c. vegetable stock
1 tbsp. (2/3 oz.) butter
1 pinch of salt
1 tsp. sugar
1 tsp. lemon juice

To garnish:
2 hard-boiled eggs, diced

1¾ ozs. cooked ham and
1¾ ozs. uncooked ham per person, for exam-
    ple "Schwarzwälder Schinken" (German
    variety of hard smoked ham from the
    Black Forest)
optional: 2 ozs. Butter

Wash the asparagus, cut off any ends which may
be woody and peel the asparagus from top to
bottom with an asparagus peeler. Then you can
trim the sticks to the same length if you wish, tie
them into bunches of four with kitchen thread.
Boil the asparagus peelings in a tall asparagus
pan with the vegetable stock, the butter, salt,
sugar and lemon juice for about 10 minutes. Remove the asparagus peelings and place the asparagus sticks in the asparagus-pan insert. Simmer in the asparagus water for between 15–20
minutes (the time depends on how fresh the asparagus is).

Serving: put one portion of asparagus on each
pre-warmed plate (remove the thread) and sprinkle with chopped egg. Place the strips of ham on
the plates. Can also be served with "Kratzede"
(see next recipe).
If desired, melt more butter and pour it over the
asparagus.
Small potatoes tossed in butter or thin pancakes
also go well with this asparagus dish.

"Kratzede"
(pancakes cut in thin slices)

4 eggs
8½ ozs. plain flower
approx ¼ c. milk and some mineral water
1 pinch of salt
2–3 tbsp. clarified butter or sunflower oil
    or rape oil

For sweet "Kratzede":
1 tbsp. sugar
icing sugar

Blend eggs and flour thoroughly, preferably with
an electric kitchen machine or an electric hand
mixer to avoid any lumps. Add the liquid ingredients slowly, season with salt or sugar and mix ingredients together thoroughly – the batter should
not be too thin. Allow the batter to thicken for at
least 30 minutes.
Stir the batter again after it has been left to stand.
Coat the base of a frying pan or cast iron pan
with oil and heat up. Pour in enough batter to
cover the bottom. Fry the pancake until its surface begins to clot, then turn over, fry briefly, cutting into strips immediately with the scraper, and
continue to fry until done.
Keep the finished "Kratzede" warm and mix the
resulting strips together in the pan when you
have finished frying.

Note: Sprinkle icing sugar over sweet "Kratzede"
and serve with fruit compote for dessert.

Where does the name "Kratzede" ("scratchings")
"Chratzede", also called "Kratzed", "Durnand" or
"Dummiss" come from? While cutting the pancake into small pieces the scraper produces a
scratching sound! This dish is similar to the Austrian "Schmarrn" – no wonder, since the regions of
Breisgau, Ortenau and the Black Forest together
with the forest towns on the Upper Rhine were
once part of "Outer Austria".

Felchen, Müllerin Art
Whitefish à la meunière

Felchen, Müllerin Art

Pro Person:
1 Bodenseefelchen von ca. 250 g
wenig Zitronensaft
Salz, weißer Pfeffer, frisch gemahlen
Mehl

Zum Braten:
Butterschmalz oder Pflanzenöl

Zum Übergießen:
zerlassene Butter

Die Felchen vom Fischhändler küchenfertig vor-
bereiten lassen. Die ausgenommenen Felchen unter fließendem kalten Wasser rasch waschen und
dann trocknen.
Innen und außen salzen, pfeffern und etwa
15 Minuten kühl stellen.
Fische in Mehl wenden, das überschüssige Mehl
abklopfen und die Felchen in heißem Butterschmalz bei mittlerer Hitzezufuhr ca. 5–6 Minuten braten, mit Zitronensaft beträufeln;
In einem Töpfchen Butter zerlassen, leicht bräunen.
Felchen auf vorgewärmte Teller legen, die Butter
darüber löffeln und mit Salzkartoffeln servieren.

Zu „Felchen, Müllerin Art" passen auch sehr gut
Nüsslisalat, Rezept Seite 20 und Kartoffelsalat,
Rezept Seite 32.

Anmerkung: Bei Konstanz reicht Baden bis an
das „Schwäbische Meer". Das Felchen ist in dieser Region der beliebteste Fisch. Neben der klassi-
schen Zubereitung „Müllerin Art" gibt es Rezepte
mit Mandelbutter, gedünsteten Champignons in
Sahnesauce u. a. mehr.
Ein sehr feiner, ebenfalls sehr beliebter Fisch in
der Bodenseeregion ist eine Barschart, „Kretzer"
oder „Egli" genannt.

Gespicktes Zanderfilet auf Rahmsauerkraut

4 Zanderfilets à 150 g, gesäubert und
   getrocknet
80 g durchwachsener Speck in ca. 2 mm
   dünne Streifen geschnitten
weißer Pfeffer, frisch gemahlen
etwas Zitronensaft
2 Esslöffel Sonnenblumenöl und
1 Esslöffel Butter
1 Teelöffel Petersilie, fein gehackt

Sauerkraut:
600 g Sauerkraut, aus dem Fass (oder Dose)
2 Esslöffel Schmalz oder Pflanzenöl
1 kleine Zwiebel, gehackt

Weitere Zutaten:
siehe Seite 40, jedoch ohne Weintrauben

Rahmsauce:
2 Schalotten, fein gehackt, 10 g Butter
$1/4$ l trockener Riesling
$1/8$ l Fischfond (evtl. aus dem Glas)
200 ml saure Sahne oder Crème fraîche
Salz, weißer Pfeffer, frisch gemahlen
20–30 g eiskalte Butterstückchen

An den Zanderfilets kleine Einschnitte anbringen,
in die der Speck gesteckt wird. Würzen, mit Zitronensaft beträufeln und kühl stellen.
Sauerkraut kürzer schneiden. In einer Kasserolle
Schmalz erhitzen, die Zwiebel anschwitzen und
das Kraut zugeben; weitere Zubereitung wie auf
Seite 44 beschrieben. Für die Sauce die Schalotten in Butter anschwitzen, Riesling und Fischfond
zugießen und die Sauce auf die Hälfte einkochen.
Sahne einrühren, würzen und die Sauce cremig
einkochen. Kurz vor dem Servieren die eiskalten
Butterstückchen unterschlagen; die Sauce mit
dem Sauerkraut mischen.
Zanderfilets im erhitzten Fett von jeder Seite 2–3
Minuten braten, Butter und Petersilie zugeben,
durchschwenken; auf dem Kraut anrichten. Dazu
passen Salzkartoffeln.

Whitefish à la meunière

Per person:
  1 Lake Constance whitefish weighing
    approx. 9 ozs.
a little lemon juice
salt, white pepper, freshly ground
flour

For frying:
clarified butter (ghee) or vegetable oil

For glazing:
melted butter

Ask the fishmonger to clean and prepare the
whitefish for the kitchen. Rinse the whitefish
briefly under running water and pat dry. Sprinkle
the inside and outside with salt and pepper; keep
cool for about 15 minutes.
Turn the fish in flour, gently pat off the superflu-
ous flour and fry the fish in hot clarified butter at
medium heat for approx. 5–6 minutes.
Melt the butter in a small pot until brown. Sprinkle with lemon.
Place the whitefish on warm plates, glaze with
the butter and serve with boiled potatoes.
You can serve this dish with "Nüsslisalat" (lamb's-
lettuce salad), recipe see page 21 and potato
salad, recipe see page 33.

Note: Baden reaches the so-called "Swabian Sea"
(Lake Constance) at Constance. Whitefish is the
most popular fish in this area. Apart from this traditional preparation à la meunière, other recipes
include almond butter, steamed mushrooms in a
cream sauce and many more variations.

A very exquisite fish, also very popular in the region of Lake Constance, is a kind of perch called
"Kretzer" or "Egli".

Larded fillet of zander on creamed sauerkraut

$5^1/_2$ ozs. zander each, cleaned and dried
  3 ozs. unsalted streaky bacon cut into very
    thin slices
white pepper, freshly ground
some lemon juice
  2 tbsp. sunflower oil and 1 tbsp. butter
  1 tbsp. parsley, finely chopped

Sauerkraut:
$1^1/_4$ lbs. sauerkraut, from the traditional
    wooden cask, alternatively out of a tin
  2 tbsp. clarified butter or vegetable oil
  1 small onion, chopped
next ingredients:
see page 41, without grapes

Cream sauce:
  2 shallots, finely chopped
  1 tbsp. butter
  $1/_2$ c. dry, white wine (German Riesling)
  $1/_4$ c. fish stock (possibly out of the jar)
  7 ozs. sour cream or crème fraiche
salt, white pepper, freshly ground
$2/_3$–1 oz. ice-cold pieces of butter

Make some cuts in the zander and thread the bacon through the cuts. Season, sprinkle the lemon
juice over the fish and keep in a cool place.
Cut the Sauerkraut into shorter pieces. Melt the
clarified butter in a casserole, fry the onion gently
until soft but not brown and add the sauerkraut.
For the finish see page 45. For the sauce, gently fry
the shallots in butter until soft but not brown, add
the fish stock and wine and boil until half of the
liquid has evaporated. Stir in the cream, season and
boil until smooth. Beat in the ice-cold butter shortly
before serving. Mix the sauerkraut with the sauce.
Heat the oil until hot and fry the fillets of zander
for 2–3 minutes each side, add parsley and toss
very gently. Side dish: boiled potatoes.

Schäufele mit Kartoffelsalat
"Schäufele" with potato salad

Schäufele mit Kartoffelsalat   Kartoffelsalat

Für 6 Portionen

1 kg gepökelte und leicht angeräucherte
Schweineschulter
$1/2$ l trockener Weißwein oder trockener
Spätburgunder Weißherbst
1 Zwiebel, geschält, mit 2 Nelken gespickt
1 Gewürzsäckchen, bestehend aus:
je 6 Pfefferkörnern und Wacholderbeeren
1 Lorbeerblatt und wenig Thymian

In einem großen Topf etwa einen Liter Wasser erhitzen, den Wein zugießen, einmal aufkochen lassen und das Schäufele einlegen. Spickzwiebel und
Gewürzsäckchen zugeben und das Fleisch bei
aufgelegtem Deckel garziehen lassen – nicht kochen. Nach etwa 1–$1 1/2$ Stunden das Fleisch aus
dem Sud nehmen, in Scheiben schneiden und auf
eine vorgewärmte Servierplatte legen. Als Beilagen Kartoffel- und Nüsslisalat, Seite 20, reichen.

Anmerkung: Schäufele, auch Schüfele genannt,
kann auch mit Bratkartoffeln oder Kartoffelstock
und Sauerkraut serviert werden. Auch in Kombi-
nation mit sauer angemachten lauwarmen Linsen
schmeckt das Schulterstück hervorragend.

Variation: Der Kochsud kann noch mit klein ge-
schnittenen Gemüsen wie Gelbe Rübe, Lauch und
Sellerie angereichert werden. Statt Thymian können auch Korianderkörner verwendet werden.

Für 6 Portionen

$1 1/2$ kg festkochende Kartoffeln, möglichst
eine schmale, längliche Sorte –
im Badischen „Mäusle" genannt
etwas Kümmelsamen

**Beiguss – das ist die alte Bezeichnung für
Salatsauce:**

1 Teelöffel sehr fein geschnittene Zwiebeln
1 Esslöffel Salz, Pfeffer, frisch gemahlen
$1/4$ bis $3/8$ l gut gewürzte Fleischbrühe – die
Menge richtet sich nach der Aufnahme-
fähigkeit der Kartoffeln
ein paar Tropfen Maggiwürze (Original: Badische Küche von Wundt)
3–4 Esslöffel heller Weinessig
4 Esslöffel Sonnenblumen- oder Rapsöl
nach Belieben: Schnittlauchröllchen

Die Kartoffeln unter Zugabe von etwas Kümmelsamen nicht zu weich kochen. Noch warm schälen und in etwa messerrückendicke Scheiben
schneiden; in eine große Schüssel geben. Die
Salatsauce anrühren, über die Kartoffelscheiben
gießen und den Salat entweder durch Schütteln
der Schüssel mit der Sauce vermischen oder die
Hände benutzen. Der Kartoffelsalat soll sehr saftig
sein; man serviert ihn lauwarm.

Anmerkung: Dieser Kartoffelsalat kann je nach
Weiterverwendung noch mit ausgebratenen
Speckstückchen oder durch Zugabe von Mayon-
naise verändert werden.

"Schäufele" (shoulder of pork) with potato salad

Serves 6

- 2 lbs. 3 ozs. cured and lightly smoked shoulder of pork
- 1 c. dry white wine or dry "Spätburgunder Weissherbst"
- 1 peeled onion, studded with 2 cloves
- 1 bouquet garni, made out of:
- 6 peppercorns and 6 juniper-berries
- 1 bay leaf and a little thyme

Pour 1 qt. water into a big saucepan and heat it up, add the wine, bring to the boil and place the meat in the pan. Add the studded onion and the bouquet garni and simmer with the lid on until the meat is tender – do not boil. Take the meat out of the stock after 1–1 1/2 hours, cut into strips and place on a pre-warmed serving dish. Serve with potato salad or "Nüsslisalat", recipe see page 21.

Note: "Schäufele", also called "Schüfele", can also be served with mashed potatoes and sauerkraut. Shoulder of pork also tastes delicious served with lukewarm lentils in vinegar.

The stock can be enriched by adding finely chopped vegetables like carrots, leeks and celeriac. You can also use coriander corns instead of thyme.

Potato salad

Serves 6

- 3 lbs. 6 ozs. firm-boiling potatoes, if possible a thin and long variety – called "Mäusle" in Baden

"Beiguss" – this is the old term for salad dressing:

- 1 tsp. finely chopped onion
- 1 tbsp. salt, pepper, freshly ground
- 1/2 to 1 c. well seasoned meat stock – the right amount depends on the capacity of absorption of the potatoes
- some drops of "Maggi" seasoning (the original brand used in Baden cuisine is Wundt, Knorr's "Maggi" provides an equivalent)
- 3–4 tbsp. white-wine vinegar
- 4 tbsp. sunflower oil or rape oil
- if desired: chopped chives

Boil the potatoes until just tender. Peel them still warm and cut into knife-thin slices; put into a big bowl. Mix the dressing, pour over the potatoes and mix together either by shaking the bowl or mixing it with your hands. The potato salad must be very juicy; serve lukewarm.

Note: Roasted chopped bacon or mayonnaise can be added to this potato salad, depending on its intended purpose, to create a little variety.

Badisches Samstagsessen
Baden Saturday meal

Badisches Samstagsessen

800–1000 g Rindfleisch, zum Sieden geeignet,
früher Ochsenfleisch, z. B. Zwerchrippe oder
  Brustkern oder Tafelspitz
  3 l Fleischbrühe oder
  3 l Wasser und 2 Esslöffel Salz
  1 Bund Suppengrün, geputzt
  1 Zwiebel, halbiert und auf der Herdplatte
  oder in einer Pfanne ohne Fett auf der
  Schnittseite gebräunt
  1 Gelbe Rübe, geputzt und halbiert
das Grüne von 1 Lauchstange
einige Kohlblätter oder Erbsenschoten –
  je nach Saison
1–2 Lorbeerblätter
  1 Zweig Liebstöckel (Maggikraut)

Meerrettichsauce:
  20 g Butter, 15 g Weizenmehl
je 1/4 l Fleischbrühe und Milch
  1/2 Stange frischer Meerrettich
  2 Scheiben entrindetes Weißbrot, zerzupft
  Salz und Pfeffer, frisch gemahlen
Je 1 Prise Muskat und Zucker
  etwas Zitronensaft

Beilagen: Bouillonkartoffeln*
Meerrettichsauce, Preiselbeeren

Fleischbrühe oder Salzwasser zum Kochen bringen, Fleisch, Suppengrün und alle anderen Einla-
gen zugeben und das Rindfleisch in etwa einein-
halb Stunden knapp unter dem Siedepunkt
garziehen lassen.
Fleisch aus der Brühe nehmen und in Scheiben
schneiden. Mit den Bouillonkartoffeln – Kartoffel-
stückchen werden mit Gelbe Rüben-Würfel und
Lauchstreifen in Fleischbrühe etwa 15 Minuten
gegart – sowie der Meerrettichsauce servieren.

---

* In den Monaten ohne „r", also Mai bis August, wenn es
keinen frischen Meerrettich gibt, wurden früher Rahm-
kartoffeln serviert.

Für die Meerrettichsoße in der erhitzten Butter
das Mehl hellgelb anschwitzen. Brühe und Milch
zugießen, gut verquirlen, damit es keine Klümpchen gibt. Den Meerrettich dazureiben und die
Brotkrümel unterziehen. Mit Salz, Pfeffer, Muskat
und Zitronensaft würzen und kurz vor dem Servieren mit dem Pürierstab aufschlagen.

Anmerkung: Die Beilagen zum Samstagsessen
können variieren; sehr beliebt ist Rahnen-Gemüse
(Rote Bete), in feine Scheiben oder Stifte geschnitten und in Butter durchgeschwenkt. Im
Frühsommer kann das Fleisch auch mit Spargel
oder Erbsenschoten umlegt werden. Gerne werden auch Perlzwiebelchen, Essiggurken, in Essig
eingemachte süßsaure Zwetschgen, Rezept Seite
48, und Preiselbeerkompott dazu gereicht.
Ochsenfleisch erhält man heute eher seltener
beim Metzger; die preiswerten Stücke werden ge-
klopft, falls nötig entbeint und mit Küchengarn
umwickelt. Man garte in einer Knochenbrühe, der
nach und nach Gemüse der Saison sowie kleine
Kartoffeln beigegeben wurden.

Übrig gebliebenes Fleisch kann mit angebratenen
Zwiebelringen, gewürzt mit Salz und Pfeffer mit
Bauernbrot zu Tisch gegeben werden.

Das Samstagsessen gab es früher u. a. deshalb,
weil man am Sonntag die Brühe für die viel-
geliebte Nudelsuppe brauchte.

Baden Saturday meal

1 lb. 12 ozs. – 2 lb. 4 ozs. beef suitable for boiling, formerly ox meat, e. g. ribs or breast or boiled fillet of ox
3 qt. meat stock or 3 qt. water and 2 tbsp. salt
1 bunch mixed soup vegetables, washed
1 onion, cut in half and fried in a pan without fat on the cut sides until these are brown
1 carrot, washed and cut in half
green parts of 1 leek
some cabbage leaves or green peas – depending on the season
1–2 bay leaves
1 twig of lovage (known in Germany, from its taste, as "Maggikraut")

Horseradish sauce

$2/3$ oz. butter, $1/2$ oz. plain flour
$1/2$ c. meat stock and $1/2$ c. milk
$1/2$ stem of fresh horseradish
2 slices white bread without the crust, plucked into small pieces
salt and pepper, freshly ground
1 pinch each of nutmeg and sugar
some lemon juice

Serve with: boiled potatoes (cooked together with vegetables)*, horseradish sauce, cranberries.

---

* In months without an "r", i.e. May to August, when no fresh horseradish is available, it used to be customary to serve potatoes in a cream sauce.

Bring stock or salted water to the boil, put the meat in, add all other ingredients and simmer at a low heat for $1\frac{1}{2}$ hours – do not boil! The temperature should be just below boiling point. Take the meat out of the stock, cut it into slices. Add the boiled potatoes (cooked with diced carrots and leek slices for 15 minutes) and serve the horseradish sauce.

To prepare the horseradish sauce, heat the butter, add the flour to form a light-coloured roux, stir in the stock and milk. Add the grated horseradish and bread, season to taste and stir briefly with a mixer just before serving.

Note: The vegetables served with the Saturday meal can vary; beetroot is very popular, cut in fine slices or sticks and sauté-ed in butter. In early summer the meat can also be garnished with asparagus or green peas. Also tastes delicious with pearl onions, pickled gherkins or sweet-sour plums, see recipe p. 49, and cranberry compote. Nowadays it is not very easy to get ox meat at the butcher's; the low-priced pieces get beaten, boned if necessary and rolled before being tied together with kitchen thread. The meat was cooked in a bone stock and vegetables of the season and small potatoes were gradually added.

Any meat left over can be served on rustic bread with fried onions, seasoned with salt and pepper.

One of the reasons why this meal used to be prepared on Saturdays is because the stock was needed on Sundays for the region's beloved noodle soup.

Fasan Winzer Art
Winzer's pheasant

Fasan, Winzer Art

1 junger Fasan von ca. 1 kg Gewicht
6 Wacholderbeeren
Salz und Pfeffer, frisch gemahlen
2 Scheiben frischer grüner oder durchwachsener Speck

Weinsauerkraut:
400 g Sauerkraut, möglichst aus dem Fass
200 ml trockener Weißwein
2–3 Wacholderbeeren, 1 Lorbeerblatt
20 g Butter
150 g frische grüne Weintrauben, entkernt
40 g Butter

Den Fasan von außen und innen waschen und trocknen. Die Wacholderbeeren zerdrücken, mit Salz und Pfeffer mischen und den Fasan damit innen und außen einreiben. Die Fasanenbrust mit den Speckscheiben bedecken und den Vogel mit Küchengarn binden; darauf achten, dass auch die Keulen eng am Körper liegen. Den Backofen auf 250 °C Grad vorheizen.
Eine Bratreine mit wenig Wasser gefüllt einschieben, den Fasan auf einem Rost über der Reine etwa 10–15 Minuten anbraten, einmal wenden. Dann die Temperatur auf 200 °C Grad zurücknehmen und den Fasan unter öfterem Bepinseln mit der Bratflüssigkeit ca. 40 Minuten braten.
Das Sauerkraut etwas kürzer schneiden und unter Zugabe von Wein und Gewürzen ca. 50 Minuten köcheln. Vor Garende etwas Butter unter das Kraut ziehen. Die halbierten und entkernten Weintrauben in Butter heiß schwenken; mit dem Sauerkraut zu dem tranchierten Fasan servieren. Dazu passen Salzkartoffeln.

Anmerkung: Man kann den Fasan auch auf einen Grillspieß stecken und im Backofen bei 210 °C Grad ca. 35–40 Minuten braten.

Geröstete Kutteln (Kaldaunen) – Geröstete Sülz

1 kg vorgekochte Sülz (Kutteln)
60 g Butterschmalz oder
30 g Butter und 3 Esslöffel Pflanzenöl
2 Zwiebeln oder
4 Schalotten, fein gehackt
Salz und Pfeffer, frisch gemahlen
1 Teelöffel frisch gepresster Zitronensaft oder
1 Esslöffel trockener Riesling
evtl. etwas Fleischbrühe
1 Teelöffel Petersilie, sehr fein gehackt

Die vorgekochte Sülz in lauwarmem Wasser waschen, trocken tupfen und in schmale Streifen schneiden. In einem Topf – möglichst aus Gusseisen – das Fett erhitzen, Zwiebeln darin goldgelb anschwitzen, die Kuttelstreifen zugeben und anrösten. Würzen, Zitronensaft oder Wein zugeben, umrühren und, falls die Kutteln zu trocken erscheinen, etwas Fleischbrühe angießen. Auf einer vorgewärmten Servierplatte anrichten. Mit Petersilie bestreut zu Tisch geben.
Dazu schmeckt Holzofenbrot.

Anmerkung: Die Sülz wird auch gern wie im Rezept „Saure Leberli" auf Seite 44 beschrieben zubereitet: Sülz mit Zwiebeln anbraten, mit Mehl bestäuben und mit Brühe oder Bratensauce ablöschen. Mit Salz, Pfeffer, Weinessig würzen und mit Tomatenmark geschmacklich abrunden.

Vintner's pheasant

1 young pheasant weighing approx. 2 lbs.
   3 ozs.
6 juniper berries
salt and pepper, freshly ground
   2 slices fresh or streaky bacon

Wine sauerkraut:

14 ozs. sauerkraut, preferably out of a
   wooden cask
just under $^1/_2$ c. dry white wine
2–3 juniper berries, 1 bay leaf
 $^2/_3$ oz. butter
$5^1/_2$ ozs. fresh green seedless grapes
$1^1/_2$ ozs. butter

Wash and dry the pheasant inside and out. Crush the juniper berries, mix them with salt and pepper and rub the outside and inside of the fowl with them. Cover the breast of the pheasant with bacon rashers and tie the fowl together with kitchen thread; make sure that the thighs are bound close against the body. Pre-heat the oven to approx. 475 °F.
Place a roasting dish containing a little water in the oven and roast the pheasant on a grid over the roasting tray for about 10–15 minutes, turning once. Then reduce the temperature to approx. 400 °F and roast the pheasant, basting it frequently with the liquid resulting from the roasting, for about 40 minutes. Cut the sauerkraut into slightly shorter strips and simmer for about 50 minutes, adding wine and juniper berries and the bay leaf. Blend a little butter with the sauerkraut before it has finished cooking. Remove the pips from the halved grapes and stir them about in butter until hot; serve with the sauerkraut and the carved pheasant. Boiled potatoes go well with this dish.

Note: The pheasant can also be roasted on a grilling spit in the oven for between 35 and 40 minutes at approx 420 °F.

Roast tripe – "Geröstete Sülz"

2 lbs. 3 ozs. pre-cooked tripe
2 ozs. clarified butter or
1 oz. butter and 3 tbsp. vegetable oil
2 onions or 4 shallots, finely chopped
salt and pepper, freshly ground
1 tsp. freshly pressed lemon juice or
1 tbsp. dry Riesling
   some meat stock
1 tsp. parsley, very finely chopped

Wash the pre-cooked tripe in lukewarm water, pat dry and cut into narrow strips. Heat the fat in a pan – preferably a cast-iron one – fry the onions until they are golden brown, add the strips of tripe and fry lightly. Add seasoning, lemon juice or wine and some meat stock stir and arrange on a heated serving dish. Serve garnished with parsley. Bread baked in a wood-burning oven tastes delicious with this dish.

Note: Tripe is often served as described in the recipe for "Sour liver" on page 45: fry the tripe lightly with the onions, sprinkle with flour and quench with broth or gravy. Season with salt, pepper, vinegar and add tomato purée to taste.

Saure Leberli mit Brägeli
Sour liver with "Brägeli"

Saure Leberli mit Brägeli

Brägeli – Brägele

600 g Kalbsleber, gehäutet
20 g Butter
1 Esslöffel Sonnenblumenöl
1 Zwiebel, sehr fein gehackt
2 Esslöffel gebräuntes Mehl
1 Esslöffel Weinessig und
3 Esslöffel Rotwein
oder ¹/₈ l trockener Weißwein und
4 Esslöffel süße Sahne
Salz und Pfeffer, frisch gemahlen
knapp ¹/₄ l Bratensauce oder Kalbsfond
nach Belieben: 1 Becher saure Sahne (125 g)

Die Kalbslebern trocken tupfen und entweder in zentimeterdicke Streifen oder Blättchen schneiden. Butter und Öl in einer Pfanne erhitzen, die Zwiebeln darin anschwitzen. Die Leberstreifen zugeben, unter Rühren anbraten und mit dem Mehl bestäuben. Weinessig und Rotwein oder Weißwein und Sahne angießen und würzen. Bratensauce oder Kalbsfond unterziehen und die Lebern noch 2–3 Minuten durchziehen lassen.
Nach Belieben kurz vor dem Servieren noch verquirlte saure Sahne unterziehen (nur bei Verwendung von Weinessig und Rotwein).

Anmerkung: Noch heute werden Innereien, speziell im Schwarzwald, traditionell zubereitet. Aus verschiedenen Kalbsinnereien wie Leber, Lunge, Milz und Herz besteht das „Röschele", früher nach dem Kirchgang im Gasthof neben der Kirche zum Frühschoppen serviert. Auch Kalbsbries kann man noch auf der Speisekarte finden: das gewässerte und gesäuberte Bries wird mit einer Spickzwiebel etwa 20 Minuten sanft gegart, dann gehäutet, in Scheiben geschnitten und in einer Butter-Wein-Sauce serviert – meist in Begleitung von „Buebespitzle" (gekochte Kartoffeln, vermischt mit Ei, Mehl, Salz und Muskat zu fingerdicken Röllchen geformt und in Salzwasser gekocht; anschließend in Schmalz gebraten).

800 g rohe Kartoffeln, geschält (eine festkochende Sorte bevorzugen)
20 g Schmalz und
30 g Butter
1 kleine Zwiebel, fein gehackt
Salz und Pfeffer, frisch gemahlen

nach Belieben: Schnittlauchröllchen
oder fein gehackte Petersilie

Die Kartoffeln in etwa 3 mm dicke Scheiben schneiden. In einer Pfanne mit dickem Boden – möglichst eine Eisenpfanne verwenden – einen Teil des Fetts erhitzen und nur so viel Kartoffelscheiben einfüllen, dass nur eine Lage den Pfannenboden bedeckt. Werden zu viele Scheiben eingefüllt, können die Kartoffeln nicht knusprig werden. Kartoffelscheiben wenden, einige Zwiebelwürfel zugeben, weiterbraten. Gebratene Kartoffeln warm halten. Alle Kartoffelscheiben auf diese Art – bei nicht zu großer Hitzezufuhr – braten. Zuletzt alles vermischen und würzen.
Nach Belieben mit Schnittlauch oder Petersilie bestreut servieren.

Anmerkung: Werden im Herbst und Winter Gänse geschlachtet, kann man das frische Gänsefett langsam in einem Topf auslassen (zum Aromatisieren kann man Majoran- oder Thymianblättchen zugeben). Die entstehenden Grieben können klein gehackt unter die fertigen Brägeli gemischt werden. Sehr lecker schmecken sie auch auf frisch gebackenem Brot. In manchen Gegenden werden sie zu Apfelkompott gereicht.

Sour liver with "Brägeli"

"Brägeli" – "Brägele"

1 ¹/₄ lbs. calf's liver, with the skin removed
²/₃ oz. butter
1 tbsp. sunflower oil
1 onion, very finely chopped
2 tbsp. browned flour
1 tbsp. wine vinegar and 3 tbsp. red wine
or ¹/₂ c. dry white wine and 4 tbsp. of cream
salt and pepper, freshly ground
just under ¹/₂ c. gravy or veal stock
if desired: 1 tub of sour cream (4 ozs.)

1 lb. 12 ozs. raw potatoes, peeled
(a firm-boiling variety is preferable)
²/₃ oz. dripping and 1 oz. butter
1 small onion, finely chopped
salt and pepper, freshly ground
if desired: cut chives
or finely chopped parsley

Pat the calf's livers dry and cut either into strips one centimetre thick or leaves. Heat the butter and oil in a pan and fry the chopped onion until soft but not brown. Add the strips of liver, stir-fry and dredge with the flour. Add wine vinegar and red wine or white wine and cream, then season. Blend in the gravy or veal stock and leave the liver in the mixture for another 2–3 minutes to allow the flavours to blend.
If desired, blend in the lightly whipped sour cream before serving (only if wine vinegar and red wine are used).

Note: Offal is still prepared in the traditional way in Baden, especially in the Black Forest. "Röschele", once served with the morning glass of wine ("Frühschoppen") at the inn beside the church after the service, is made with various items of veal offal such as liver, lung, pancreas and heart. Veal sweetbreads are still to be found on menus: the soaked and cleaned sweetbreads are gently simmered with an onion spiked with cloves for about 20 minutes. The skins are then removed, the sweetbreads cut into slices and served in a butter-wine sauce – usually accompanied by "Buebespitzle" (finger-thick noodles). These are made from boiled, grated potatoes, mixed with egg, flour, salt and nutmeg; cooked in salted water, fried in ghee and served.

Cut the potatoes into slices about 3 mm thick. Heat some of the fat in a thick-bottomed pan – preferably made of cast iron – and add enough potato slices to just cover the bottom with one layer. If too many slices are added, the potatoes cannot become crispy. Turn the potato slices, add some diced onion, keep the fried potatoes warm. Fry all the potato slices in this way – without using too much heat. Finally mix all the slices together and season. If desired, serve sprinkled with chives or parsley.

Note: When geese are killed in autumn and winter, the fresh goose grease can be slowly rendered down and stored in a pot (add aroma with a few leaves of marjoram or thyme). The greaves that result can be chopped small and mixed with the finished "Brägeli". "Brägeli" are also very tasty on freshly-baked bread. In some areas they are served with apple compote.

Bibbeliskäs mit Pellkartoffeln

*"Bibbeliskäs" with potatoes
boiled in their skins*

Bibbeliskäs mit Pellkartoffeln

800 g Bibbeliskäs – Quark, falls möglich vom
    Bauern oder selbst hergestellt
1 Knoblauchzehe, durch die Presse gedrückt
    oder feinst gehackt
2 Schalotten, fein gehackt
1 Bund Schnittlauch, fein geschnitten
3–4 Esslöffel dicke saure Sahne oder Crème
    double
Salz und Pfeffer, frisch gemahlen
Pro Person 3–4 Pellkartoffeln mit etwas
    Kümmel gekocht

Bibbeliskäs in eine große Schüssel geben, alle an-
deren Zutaten einrühren. Oder den Quark mit
Sahne, Salz und Pfeffer verrühren und Knoblauch,
Schalotten und Schnittlauch in kleinen Schüsseln
separat dazu servieren.
Pellkartoffeln dazu reichen, die im Frühjahr als
„Neue Kartoffeln" durchaus mit der Schale ver-
zehrt werden können.

Anmerkung: Der Begriff „Bibbeliskäs" wird auch
im nahe gelegenen Elsass. verwendet. Er bezeichnet die frisch geschlüpften Küken, die „Bibbeli"
Ob man die wohl damit gefüttert hat? Vielleicht
in den wohlhabenderen Gegenden. Gewöhnlich
hat man die Küken mit einem Brei aus altbackenem Brot, Eigelb und Milch aufgepäppelt.

Die einstige Wirtin des Feldberger Hofs, Fanny
Mayer, deren Name im 19. Jh. für die Badische
Gastlichkeit stand, erzählte aus ihren Dienstjahren
in einem Basler Patrizierhaus, sie habe einmal für
die „Bibbeli" ein „Bäbbli" aus altbackenem Weißbrot, Milch und Eigelb zubereitet. Das habe eine
sehr reiche Verwandte der Familie als Verschwen-
dung bezeichnet und es daraufhin selbst ver-
speist. Auf Fanny Mayers Frage, mit was sie denn
nun die „Bibbeli" füttern solle, meinte die Basle-
rin, die sollten doch gefälligst an der Alten sau-
gen.

Süßsauer eingelegte Zwetschgen

1 kg Zwetschgen
$^1/_2$ l guter Rotweinessig
500 g feiner Zucker
2 Lorbeerblätter
4–5 Gewürznelken
1 Stückchen Stangenzimt
0,2 l Rotwein

Die Zwetschgen entstielen, mit einem Tuch abrei-
ben, aber nicht waschen, auch nicht entsteinen.
Den Essig mit Zucker, den Gewürzen und Wein
aufkochen, von der Herdplatte nehmen und einige Minuten ziehen lassen; abkühlen lassen. Die
Zwetschgen in ein hohes Einmachglas oder in
einen Steinguttopf einfüllen und mit der Flüssigkeit übergießen; sie müssen davon bedeckt sein.
Zum Durchziehen etwa einen Monat im kühlen
Keller aufbewahren.

Anmerkung: Die Zwetschgen können auch im
Einmachglas sterilisiert werden.

"Bibbeliskäs" (quark) with potatoes boiled in their skins

1lb. 12 ozs. quark, if possible from the farm or
   home-made
  1 clove of garlic, crushed in a garlic press or
   very finely chopped
  2 shallots, finely chopped
  1 bunch of chives, finely cut
3–4 tbsp. thick sour cream or crème double
salt and pepper, freshly ground
3–4 potatoes boiled in their skins per person,
   boiled with a few caraway seeds

Put the "Bibbeliskäs" in a large bowl and stir in
all the other ingredients. Or mix the quark with
the cream, salt and pepper, serving the garlic,
shallots and chives separately in small bowls.
Serve with potatoes boiled in their skins which, in
the case of spring "new potatoes", can also be
eaten.

Note: The term "Bibbeliskäs" is also used in
neighbouring Alsace. Was it perhaps fed to the
freshly-hatched chicks, or "Bibbeli"?. In the
wealthier regions, perhaps. Usually, the chicks
were fed up with a pap of stale bread, egg yolk
and milk.

The former landlady of the "Feldberger Hof",
Fanny Mayer, who was synonymous with Baden
hospitality in the 19th century, once told that during her years of service in a patrician household in
Basle she once prepared for the "Bibbeli" a "Bäbbli" (pap) made of stale white bread, milk and
egg yolk. An extremely rich relative of the family
pointed out what a waste it was and promptly
ate the pap herself! When Fanny Mayer asked
what she was to feed to the "Bibbeli" now, the
old lady said they should suck the milk of the old
hen for all she cared!

Sweet-sour preserved plums

  2 lbs. 3 ozs. plums
  1 c. good red-wine vinegar
  1 lb. 1$^1/_2$ ozs. caster sugar
  2 bay leaves
4–5 cloves
  1 piece of cinnamon stem
$^1/_2$ c. red wine

Remove the stalks from the plums and rub them
with a cloth but do not wash them or remove the
stones. Bring the vinegar to boil with the sugar,
spice and wine, remove from the heat and allow
the flavours to blend for several minutes; allow to
cool. Put the plums into a tall preserving jar or an
earthenware jar and pour the liquid over them;
they must be covered with liquid. Store in a cool
cellar for about a month to allow the flavours to
blend.

Note: The plums can also be sterilized in the preserving jar.

Zwetschgenweihe
"Zwetschgenweihe" – Plum flan

Zwetschgenweihe

Hefeteig:
200 g Mehl
15 g frische Hefe
2 Esslöffel Zucker
ca. $\frac{1}{8}$ l lauwarme Milch
40–60 g Butter
1 Prise Salz
1 kleines Ei

Belag:
1 kg oder mehr Zwetschgen – senkrecht
gestellt braucht man mehr – entsteint

Zum Bestreuen:
Haferflocken oder Zwiebackmehl
Zucker und Zimt

Mehl in eine Backschüssel geben, in die Mitte
eine Vertiefung drücken. Die Hefe mit etwas Zucker, wenig Mehl und Milch anrühren und in die
Vertiefung gießen. Etwas Mehl darüber stäuben
und die Schüssel zudecken. Wenn die Mehldecke
aufreißt, alle übrigen Zutaten einarbeiten und den
Teig solange kneten, bis er sich vom Schüsselbo-
den löst. Auf Backblechgröße ausrollen. Ein Back-
blech einfetten und die Teigplatte darauf legen.
Nochmals gehen lassen.
Inzwischen die Zwetschgen entsteinen und zur
Hälfte einschneiden. Den Teig mit Haferflocken
oder Bröseln bestreuen und mit den Zwetschgen
dicht belegen. Man darf keinen Teig mehr sehen.
Den Kuchen bei 180 °C in 40–50 Minuten ausbacken, lauwarm abkühlen lassen und dann mit Zucker und Zimt bestreuen.

Anmerkung: Früher wurde die Weihe am Back-
tag aus den Resten des Brotteigs hergestellt und
war dann, meist mit einer am Vorabend gekoch-
ten Suppe, das Mittagessen. Weil diese Teigreste
sparsam verwendet, und daher sehr dünn ausge-
rollt wurden, nannte man die Weihe auch „Dünne".

Kerscheplotzer

800 g süße dunkle Kirschen
6 altbackene Milchbrötchen
ca. $\frac{1}{4}$ l Milch

Creme:
4 Eier, getrennt
100 g Zucker
80 g Butter
1 Gläschen Kirschwasser
1 Prise Salz

Nach Belieben:
50 g Mandelstifte oder
50 g klein gehackte Haselnüsse

Für die Form:
Butter, Semmelbrösel

Zum Bestäuben:
Puderzucker

Die Kirschen waschen, abtropfen lassen und entsteinen. Die Brötchen in schmale Scheiben schneiden und in der Milch einweichen. Aus den Eigel-
ben, Zucker, Butter und Kirschwasser eine Creme
rühren. Mandelstifte oder Nüsse darunter rühren.
Die Eiweiße mit etwas Salz steif schlagen, unter
die Creme ziehen. Vorsichtig mit den Kirschen
und den Brötchen vermischen und die Masse in
eine mit Butter ausgefettete und mit Semmelbrö-
seln ausgestreute Form einfüllen. Im vorgeheizten
Backofen bei ca. 180 °C etwa 1 Stunde backen.
Den Kerscheplotzer mit Puderzucker bestäuben
und sofort servieren.

Anmerkung: Kerscheplotzer, oder *Chrisiplotzer*
und mancherorts auch *Kirschenmichel*, kann auch
mit Sauerkirschen und Schwarzbrotscheiben zubereitet werden, dann die Kruste abschneiden. Das
Gericht war früher zusammen mit einer Suppe
(voraus serviert) ein beliebtes Wochenendessen.

"Zwetschgenweihe" – Plum flan

Leavened dough:

 7 ozs. plain flour
 $1/_2$ oz. fresh yeast
 2 tbsp. sugar
approx. $1/_4$ c. lukewarm milk
$1^1/_2$ – 2 ozs. butter
 1 pinch of salt
 1 small egg

Filling:

$2^1/_4$ lbs. (or more*) plums, with stones removed

For sprinkling on top:
oats or rusk crumbs, sugar and cinnamon

Put the flour in a mixing bowl, make a depression
in the middle. Mix the yeast with some sugar, a
little flour and milk and pour into the depression.
Sprinkle a little flour over it and cover the bowl.
When the covering of flour breaks up, work in all
the other ingredients and knead the dough until
it lifts off the base of the bowl. Roll out the
dough the size of a baking tray. Grease or line a
baking tray with baking paper and place the
dough on it. Allow the dough to rise again.
In the meantime, remove the stones from the
plums and halve or slit them. Sprinkle oats or rusk
crumbs and cover generously with the plums. No
pastry should be visible.
Bake the cake for between 40 and 50 minutes at
350 °F, let it cool until lukewarm and then dredge
with sugar and cinnamon.

Note: In former times, the "Weihe" was made on
baking day out of any remnants of the bread
dough and was then eaten as lunch, usually with
a soup made the previous evening. Because these
remnants of dough were used sparingly and thus
rolled out very thin, the "Weihe" was also called
"Dünne" ("the thin one").

"Kerscheplotzer" – Cherry Pudding

Cream filling:

 4 eggs, yolks and whites separate
$3^1/_2$ ozs. sugar
 3 ozs. butter
 1 liqueur glass of "Kirschwasser" (cherry
 schnapps)
 1 pinch of salt

$1^3/_4$ ozs. almonds, cut lengthways into slivers,
 or $1^3/_4$ ozs. chopped hazelnuts

For the tray:
butter, breadcrumbs

For dredging:
icing sugar

Wash the cherries, let them drip dry and remove
the stones. Cut the bread rolls in narrow strips and
soften in the milk. Whisk the yolks, sugar, butter
and Kirschwasser to a creamy texture. Mix in the
almond slivers or nuts. Whip the egg whites stiff
with a little salt, blend into the cream. Carefully
mix with the cherries and the rolls and put the mixture into a baking tray greased with butter and
lightly lined with breadcrumbs. Bake in a pre-heated oven for about 1 hour at approx. 350 °F. Sprinkle icing sugar over the "Kerscheplotzer" and serve
immediately.

Note: "Kerscheplotzer" or "Chrisiplotzer" and
also named "Kirschenmichel" can also be made
with sour cherries and slices of black bread if the
crusts are removed. This dish used to be a popular
weekend meal in combination with soup (served
first).

Schwarzwälder Kirschtorte
Black Forest Cherry Gâteau

Schwarzwälder Kirschtorte

Für eine Tortenform von 28 cm Durchmesser
für 16 Tortenstücke

Schokoladenbiskuit:

   4 Eiweiß,
   4 Esslöffel kaltes Wasser
250 g Zucker
   1 Päckchen Vanillezucker
   4 Eigelbe
125 g feines Weizenmehl
125 g Speisestärke
   1 Teelöffel Backpulver
   50 g Kakaopulver oder
   80 g geriebene Bitterschokolade

Eiweiß mit Wasser sehr steif schlagen, Zucker und
Vanillezucker einrieseln lassen, kurz unterschlagen
und die Eigelbe darunter ziehen. Mehl mit Speisestärke und Backpulver sowie Kakao oder Schokola-
de vermischen und vorsichtig unter die Eiweißmas-
se heben. Den Teig in eine nur am Boden gefettete
oder mit Backpapier ausgelegte Springform füllen
und im vorgeheizten Backofen bei 180 °C etwa 35
Minuten backen. Nach dem Erkalten zweimal
durchschneiden, so dass man drei Böden erhält.

Weitere Zutaten:

750 g frische Sauerkirschen, entsteint oder
   1 Glas eingemachte Kompott-Sauer-
      kirschen ca. 480 – 500 g, gut abgetropft
   2 Esslöffel Zucker
   2 Gläschen Kirschwasser
$^1/_2$ l süße Sahne (Rahm)
   4 Blatt weiße Gelatine, eingeweicht und
      ausgedrückt – wenn die Torte einige Zeit
      stehen soll

   50 g Schokoladenspäne oder Borkenschoko-
      lade zum Bestreuen und für den Rand

Die Sauerkirschen mit Zucker und etwa 1 Glas
Kirschwasser vermischen und gut durchziehen lassen. Den untersten Tortenboden mit etwas Kirschwasser beträufeln, einen Teil der Sauerkirschen
gleichmäßig darauf verteilen. Die Sahne unter
Zugabe von Gelatine steif schlagen. Den zweiten
Boden auf die Sauerkirschen legen, mit Schlagsahne bestreichen, einige Kirschen darauf verteilen, ein paar zum Garnieren zurück behalten. Den
dritten Tortenboden auflegen, die restliche
Schlagsahne auf der Oberfläche und um den
Rand verteilen, evtl. einen Spritzbeutel verwenden. Auf die Tortenoberfläche 16 Tupfer spritzen,
jeweils eine Kirsche aufsetzen und die Stücke evtl.
mittels leichtem Einritzen markieren. Den Rand
und die Mitte der Oberfläche mit Schokoladen-
spänen oder Borkenschokolade bestreuen.

Anmerkung: Möchte man der Sauerkirschfüllung
mehr Stabilität verleihen, empfiehlt sich folgendes
Rezept: Kirschsaft mit kalt angerührter Speisestärke vermischen, mit wenig Zucker und etwas
Zitronensaft sowie einer Zimtstange einmal aufkochen und erkalten lassen. Die Zimtstange entfernen und die Mischung mit den Kirschen ver-
mengen.

Eines von vielen „Originalrezepten" – dieses
stammt von der in Pforzheim geborenen Koch-
buchautorin Hermine Kiehnle.

Black Forest Cherry Gâteau
One of many "original recipes"

For a flan case 28 cm in diameter
providing 16 slices of gâteau

Chocolate sponge:
     4 egg whites, 4 tbsp. of cold water
8$^1/_2$ ozs. sugar
     1 sachet of vanilla sugar
     4 egg yolks
4$^1/_4$ ozs. fine wheat flour (plain)
4$^1/_4$ ozs. cornflour
     1 tsp. baking powder
1$^1/_2$ ozs. cocoa or 3 ozs. grated dark chocolate

Whisk the egg whites with water until very stiff,
trickle in the sugar and vanilla sugar, briefly beat
together and draw in the egg yolks from below.
Mix flour with cornflour, baking powder and
cocoa and carefully lift in below the egg-white
mixture. Fill the cake mixture into a spring-clip
cake tin greased or lined with baking paper at the
bottom only and bake in a pre-heated oven for
about 35 minutes at 350°F. After the chocolate
sponge has cooled, cut it twice so that you have
three layers.

Further ingredients:
     1 lb. 10 ozs. fresh sour cherries with stones
        removed or 1 jar (just over 1 lb.) of bot-
        tled sour-cherry compote. Allow all the
        juice to drip off
     2 tbsp. sugar
     2 liqueur glasses of "Kirschwasser" (cherry
        schnapps)
     1 c. double cream
     4 leaves of white gelatine, softened and
        pressed out – if the gâteau is to be left
        for any length of time
1$^3/_4$ ozs. chocolate chips or chocolate flakes to
        sprinkle over the top and on the sides

Mix the sour cherries with sugar and about 1
liqueur glass of "Kirschwasser" and let them
blend well. Sprinkle a little "Kirschwasser" on the
bottom layer of sponge, spread one portion of
the sour cherries evenly over it. Whip the cream
stiff, adding the gelatine if required. Place the
second layer on the cherries, coat with whipped
cream, spread a few cherries over the cream but
keep a few back for ornamentation. Place the
third layer of sponge on top, spread the remain-
der of the whipped cream over the top and
around the sides using a piping bag if needed.
Pipe 16 whirls on the top, place a cherry on each
and mark the pieces by scoring lightly if desired.
Sprinkle chocolate chips or chocolate flakes on
the sides and in the middle of the top.

Note: To give the sour-cherry filling more stability,
the following recipe is to be recommended: mix
some cherry juice with a tablespoon of cornflour
mixed cold, bring to the boil once, adding a little
sugar, some lemon juice and a stem of cinnamon,
and leave to cool. Remove the cinnamon stem
and blend the mixture with the cherries.

This recipe of a Black Forest Cherry Gâteau is by
Hermine Kiehnle, a famous cookbook author,
born in Pforzheim.

Markgräfler Nusstorte
Markgräfler Nut Gâteau

Markgräfler Nusstorte

Rezept für eine Torte von ca. 24 cm Durchmesser

Füllung:

335 g Zucker, feine Qualität
ca. 300 g Walnüsse, grob gehackt
     (ersatzweise Haselnüsse)
200 ml süße Sahne (1 Becher)
2 Esslöffel flüssiger Honig

Mürbeteig für Boden und Deckel:

375 g Weizenmehl
180 g Butter
100 g feiner Zucker
1 Päckchen Vanillezucker oder Schalen-
    abrieb von $1/2$ Zitrone
1 Ei
1 Prise Salz

Weitere Zutaten:

1 Eiweiß, leicht verquirlt
1 Eigelb, verquirlt mit
2 Esslöffel süßer Sahne

Zunächst die Füllung zubereiten, da sie vor der Weiterverwendung abkühlen muss. Den Zucker in einer beschichteten Pfanne schmelzen, er soll goldfarben aber nicht braun sein. Die grob gehackten Nüsse einrühren. Wenn sie gut mit dem Zucker überzogen sind, die Sahne zugießen und den Honig zufügen. Bei sehr geringer Hitzezufuhr so lange verrühren, bis alle Zutaten sich gut verbunden haben. Von der Kochstelle nehmen und abkühlen lassen. Aus den angegebenen Zutaten rasch einen Mürbeteig kneten und etwa 30 Minuten in den Kühlschrank stellen. Die Teigmasse in zwei Portionen teilen, wobei eine Portion etwas größer sein sollte. Die größere Portion zwischen zwei Klarsichtfolien ausrollen und entweder in eine gut gefettete oder eine beschichtete Backform legen. Den Rand hochziehen. Die Füllung auf die Teigplatte geben, mit einem befeuchteten Backspatel glatt streichen. Die zweite Teigportion möglichst rund ausrollen. Den hochgezogenen Teigrand über die Füllung klappen und mit Eiweiß bestreichen. Zweite Teigplatte auflegen und den Rand gut andrücken – das Eiweiß ist der Klebestoff. Das verquirlte Eigelb auf die Oberfläche streichen und mit einer Gabel einige Male einstechen, damit der Dampf entweichen kann. Den Backofen auf ca. 200 °C vorheizen, den Kuchen auf der mittleren Schiene ca. 35 bis 40 Minuten backen. Mit einem Holzstäbchen die Garprobe machen. Den Kuchen gut auskühlen lassen, dann in Alufolie wickeln oder in eine entsprechend große Blechdose legen und mindestens eine Woche durchziehen lassen. So bleibt die Torte saftig. Die Nusstorte kann kühl gelagert einige Wochen aufbewahrt werden.

Anmerkung: Diese Nusstorte ist ein „Zuwanderer" aus der nahen Schweiz, aus dem Engadin.
Die Luxusvariante wird mit Walnüssen, die einfache Art mit Haselnüssen zubereitet.

Markgräfler Nut Gâteau

Recipe for a gâteau approx. 24 cm in diameter

Filling:

12 ozs. caster sugar
about 10 1/2 ozs. walnuts, roughly chopped
  (hazelnuts may be used instead)
7 ozs. double cream (1 tub)
2 tbsp. clear (liquid) honey

Rich short pastry for bottom and top:

13 ozs. plain flour
6 1/2 ozs. butter
3 1/2 ozs. caster sugar
1 sachet of vanilla sugar or grated peel of
  half a lemon
1 egg
1 pinch of salt

Further ingredients:

1 egg white, lightly beaten
1 egg yolk, beaten with
2 tbsp. double cream

First prepare the filling, as this has to cool down before it is needed again. Melt the sugar in a coated saucepan until it is golden yellow but not brown. Stir in the roughly chopped nuts. When they are well coated with sugar, add the cream and the honey. Mix at very low heat until all the ingredients are well blended. Remove from the stove and allow to cool. Quickly knead a sweet short pasty from the ingredients listed and place in the refrigerator for about 30 minutes. Divide the dough into two portions, one portion being slightly larger. Roll out the larger portion between two sheets of clear plastic foil and place in a baking tin that is either well-greased or coated. Raise the edge. Pour the filling on the pastry base, smooth with a moistened baking spatula. Roll out the second portion of dough as round as possible. Fold the raised edge of dough over the filling and coat with white of egg. Place the second layer of pastry on top and press the edge firmly against it – the egg white serves as glue. Spread the whipped yolk over the top and prick several times with a fork to let any steam escape. Pre-heat the oven to approx. 400°F and bake the cake for about 35 to 40 minutes on the middle grid. Test with a wooden skewer to see whether the cake is done. Allow the cake to cool thoroughly, then wrap in aluminium foil or place in a sufficiently large tin with a lid. Keep for at least a week to allow the flavours to blend. This keeps the cake moist. The nut gâteau will keep for several weeks if stored in a cool place.

Note: This nut gâteau is an "immigrant" from the Swiss Engadine region. The luxury version is prepared with walnuts, the simple version with hazelnuts.

Linzer Torte · Linz gâteau

Linzer Torte

250 g Butter
4 bis 5 Eigelbe
250 g Zucker
125 g gemahlene Mandeln
125 g gemahlene Haselnüsse
abgeriebene Schale einer Zitrone
1 Messerspitze Zimtpulver
1 Messerspitze Nelkenpulver
2 Gläschen Kirschwasser
500 g Mehl
$^1/_2$ Päckchen Backpulver
1 Glas Himbeermarmelade

Die Butter bei Zimmertemperatur etwas weich werden lassen und schaumig rühren. Ein Eigelb zum Bestreichen aufbewahren. Die restlichen Eigelbe mit dem Zucker zur Butter geben und etwa 10 Minuten rühren. Dann Mandeln, Nüsse, Zitronenschale, Zimt- und Nelkenpulver und den Schnaps hinzugeben. Das Mehl mit dem Backpulver zusammen darüber sieben und alles gut verkneten. Eine Teigkugel formen und etwa 1 Stunde an einem kühlen Ort kalt stellen. Den Teig in zwei Hälften teilen. Aus einer Teighälfte einen Boden von etwa $^1/_2$ cm Dicke ausrollen. Eine gut mit Butter eingefettete Springform damit belegen. Marmelade über den Teig streichen. Die zweite Hälfte des Teiges ebenso ausrollen und daraus etwa 1 $^1/_2$ bis 2 cm breite Streifen ausrädeln. Mit diesen Streifen die Marmelade im spitzen Winkel gitterartig belegen. Zum Schluss einen Streifen als Rand um den ganzen Kuchen legen. Das Gitter und den Rand mit dem aufbewahrten Eigelb bestreichen. Die Linzer Torte in dem auf 180°C vorgeheizten Backofen ca. 1 Stunde backen.

Die Linzer Torte sollte nach dem Backen mindestens drei Tage ruhen; je länger sie ruht, desto besser wird sie.

Fasnachtsküchle, auch „Scherben" genannt

Teig:
500 g Mehl
1 Prise Salz
150 g Butter
60 g Zucker – wer's gern süß hat, nimmt 100 g
4 Eier oder 2 ganze Eier und
3 Eigelbe
1 Päckchen Backpulver

Oder Hefeteig:
500 g Mehl
20 g Hefe
ca. $^1/_4$ l Milch
60–80 g Butter
60 g Zucker, $^1/_2$ Teelöffel Salz
1 Ei
Mehl zum Ausrollen

Zum Ausbacken:
Schmalz oder Pflanzenöl oder Butterschmalz

Zum Bestäuben:
Puderzucker evtl. vermischt mit Vanillezucker

Mehl mit Salz, Butter, Zucker, den Eiern und Backpulver mit der Küchenmaschine zu einem Teig verarbeiten. Oder aus den angegebenen Zutaten einen Hefeteig wie für Zwetschgenweihe (Seite 52) herstellen. Etwa 30 Minuten ruhen lassen. Ein Backbrett bemehlen, den Teig darauf portionsweise dünn ausrollen und mit einem Teigrädchen Rauten davon schneiden. In einer tiefen Pfanne oder in einer Fritteuse das Fett erhitzen und die Teigstücke – nicht zu viel auf einmal – einlegen und darin goldgelb ausbacken. Auf Küchenpapier abtropfen lassen und noch warm mit Puderzucker bestreut servieren.
Die Küchle schmecken am besten frisch ausgebacken!

Linz gâteau

8 1/2 ozs. butter
   4 to 5 egg yolks
8 1/2 ozs. sugar
4 1/4 ozs. ground almonds
4 1/4 ozs. ground hazelnuts
grated rind of one lemon
   1 pinch of powdered cinnamon
   1 pinch of powdered cloves
   2 liqueur glasses of "Kirschwasser" (cherry
     schnapps)
   1 lb. 1 1/2 ozs. plain flour
half a sachet of baking powder
   1 jar of raspberry jam

Allow the butter to soften at room temperature
and whisk until frothy. Keep one egg yolk for
spreading over the pastry. Add the remaining
yolks and the sugar to the butter and stir for
about 10 minutes. Then add the almonds, hazelnuts, lemon peel, powdered cinnamon and cloves
together with the schnapps. Sieve the flour mixed
with the baking powder over the mixture and
knead well. Shape the pastry into a ball and keep
in a cool place for one hour. Divide the pastry ball
into two halves. Roll one of the halves into a base
about a quarter of an inch thick. Place in a
spring-clip cake tin well greased with butter.
Spread the jam over the pastry. Roll out the other
half of the pastry and divide into strips half to
three-quarters of an inch thick with a pastry cutter. Place these strips on the jam to form a grid at
an acute angle. Finally lay one strip around the
cake to form an edge. Use the egg yolk saved to
coat the strips and the edge. Bake your Linz
gateau in a pre-heated oven for approx. one hour
at 350–365 °F.

Linz gateau should be left for at least three days
after baking. The longer it is left, the better it
tastes.

"Fasnachtsküchle"
Carnival doughnuts

Dough:
   1 lb. 1 1/2 ozs. plain flour
   1 pinch of salt
5 1/2 ozs. butter
   2 ozs. sugar – those who like it sweet
     should take 3 ozs.
   4 eggs or 2 whole eggs and 3 egg yolks
   1 sachet of baking powder

Or a leavened dough:
   1 lb. 1 1/2 ozs. plain flour
   2/3 oz. yeast
approx. 1/2 c. milk
2–3 ozs. butter
   2 ozs. sugar, 1/2 tsp. salt
   1 egg
Flour for rolling

For frying:
lard or vegetable oil or clarified butter

For dredging:
Icing sugar, mixed with vanilla sugar if desired

Mix the flour with the salt, butter, sugar, eggs
and baking powder or cream into a dough in a
kitchen mixer. Or make a leavened dough from
the ingredients listed (as for "Zwetschgenweihe",
page 53). Leave to stand for about 30 minutes.
Spread flour onto a baking board, roll out the
dough thinly in portions and cut out lozenge
shapes with a pastry cutter. Heat up the fat in a
deep frying pan or in a electric fryer (friteuse) and
pop in the pieces of dough – not too many at a
time. Fry until golden brown. Allow the fat to drip
off onto a piece of kitchen towel and serve while
still warm dredged in icing sugar. The doughnuts
taste best while they are still fresh!

Erdbeeren mit Frischkäse

*Strawberries with
Münstertal curd cheese*

Erdbeeren mit Frischkäse

Hildabrötchen

250 g Erdbeeren (1 Schale)
6 cl Schwarzwälder Kirschwasser
50 g Puderzucker

Frischkäsecreme:

350 g Frischkäse – falls möglich aus dem
Münstertal
100 ml süße Sahne
Saft und dünn abgeschälte Schale von
1/2 unbehandelten Limette oder Zitrone
1 Esslöffel flüssiger Honig

Nach Belieben:

450 g Tiefkühlblätterteig, aufgetaut, die
Scheiben halbiert und bei ca. 220°C etwa
10 Minuten gebacken

Erdbeeren waschen, entstielen und die Früchte
vierteln. In einer Schüssel mit Kirschwasser über-
gossen und mit Puderzucker bestäubt, bis zum
Servieren im Kühlschrank durchziehen lassen.
Den Frischkäse mit der Sahne verrühren, Zitrussaft
und Schale sowie den Honig zugeben und unter-
mischen. Nach Belieben Teller mit Blätterteig-
böden belegen, Erdbeeren dazulegen. Den Frischkäse in Nocken abstechen, zu den Erdbeeren
geben. Blätterteigscheiben auflegen und evtl. mit
Puderzucker bestäuben.

Anmerkung: Zu diesem Nachtisch passen geschmacklich und farblich sehr gut Zitronenmelis-
seblättchen.
Ist kein passender Frischkäse erhältlich, kann evtl.
auf Hüttenkäse, vermischt mit Sahnejoghurt oder
auch auf Ricotta ausgewichen werden.

Ergibt etwa 45 Stück

300 g Weizenmehl
150 g kalte Butterstücke (kleine Würfel)
120 g feiner Zucker, 1/2 P. Vanillezucker
1 Ei

Zum Füllen:

Hägenmark (Hagebuttenmarmelade) oder
Johannisbeermarmelade

Glasur:

125 g Puderzucker, 2–3 Esslöffel Wasser

Das Mehl auf ein Backbrett sieben. Die Butterstückchen kreisförmig darauf verteilen. Von außen
her mit dem Mehl rasch verkneten. Dann den Zucker, Vanillezucker und das Ei einarbeiten, bis eine
glatte Masse entsteht. Den Teig in Klarsichtfolie
einschlagen und etwa 30 Minuten im Kühlschrank
ruhen lassen. Den Teig portionsweise zwischen
Klarsichtfolie auf dem Backbrett etwa 1/4 cm dick
auswellen und runde Plätzchen von 5 cm Durchmesser ausstechen. Die Plätzchen auf ein gefette-
tes oder mit Backtrennpapier belegtes Blech legen
und nacheinander im vorgeheizten Backofen bei
150–170°C in etwa 18–20 Minuten hellgelb backen.
Nach dem Backen nur kurz lauwarm abkühlen lassen. Die Hälfte der Plätzchen mit Marmelade bestreichen und die andere Hälfte als Deckel auflegen. Die Oberfläche mit der Puderzuckerglasur bestreichen.

Die Hildabrötchen gehen auf die letzte Großherzo-
gin Badens zurück, die zeitlebens mit dem Auf und
Ab politischer Machtverschiebungen konfrontiert
war und an der Seite ihres Mannes, Erbgroßherzog
Friedrich II., abdanken musste, als Baden von der
Monarchie in eine Republik umgewandelt wurde.

Strawberries with Münstertal curd cheese

8 1/2 ozs. strawberries – 1 punnet
  1 small liqueur glass Black Forest
    "Kirschwasser" (cherry schnapps)
1 3/4 ozs. icing sugar

Curd-cheese cream:

  12 ozs. curd cheese – if possible, the Mün-
    stertal variety
3 1/2 ozs. double cream
juice and thinly peeled skin of half an
    untreated lime or lemon
  1 tbsp. clear honey

If desired,:

  1 lb. deep-frozen flaky pastry, thawed, slices
    halved and baked for about 10 minutes at
    approx. 430 °F

Wash the strawberries, remove the stalks and cut
into quarters. Put into a bowl, pour the
"Kirschwasser" over the fruit and dredge with icing sugar. Keep refrigerated until served to allow
the flavours to blend. Mix the curd cheese with
the cream, add the lime or lemon juice and skin
together with the honey. If desired, place flaky
pastry on the plates as a base, lay the strawberries on top and punch out stubs of curd cheese.
Place these on the strawberries. Place slices of
flaky pastry on top and dredge with icing sugar if
desired.

Note: In taste and colour, small leaves of lemon
balm go very well with this dessert. If no suitable
curd cheese can be obtained, cottage cheese
mixed with creamy yoghurt or even ricotta provide alternatives.

Hilda cookies

Makes about 45
  11 ozs. plain flour
5 1/2 ozs. pieces of butter
4 1/4 ozs. caster sugar, fragranced with vanilla
  1 egg

For filling:
Rose-hip jam or blackcurrant jam

Icing:
  4 ozs. icing sugar, 2–3 tbsp. water

Sieve the flour onto a baking board. Distribute
the pieces of butter – cut into as tiny cubes as
possible – in circles on the flour. Quickly knead
the flour and butter from outwards in – possibly
chopping together with a large knife. Then work
in the sugar and the egg until a smooth paste is
formed. Wrap the pastry in clear plastic foil and
leave in the refrigerator for about 30 minutes.
Roll out the pastry in portions between clear plastic foil on the baking board until it is 1/8 inch
thick and cut out cookie shapes about 5 cm in
diameter. Place the cookies on a baking tray that
has been greased or lined with baking paper and
bake one tray after the other in a pre-heated
oven for about 18–20 minutes at 300–345 °F until they are light gold in colour. After baking, only
allow them to cool for a short time until they are
lukewarm. Spread jam on half the cookies and
place the others on top as a lid. Coat the surface
with the icing.

Hilda cookies are named after the last Grand
Duchess of Baden, who was confronted all her
life by the ups and downs of shifts in power poli-
tics and, together with her husband, the heredi-
tary Grand Duke Friedrich II, was forced to abdi-
cate when Baden was transformed from a grand
duchy into a republic.

Z Müllen an der Post,
Tausigsappermost!
Trinkt me nit e guete Wi!
Goht er nit wie Baumöl i,
z' Müllen an der Post!

JOHANN PETER HEBEL

Baden ist da, wo der Gutedel wächst. Die Rebsorte, die der damalige Markgraf Karl Friedrich von Baden in seiner Studienzeit an der protestantischen Akademie in Lausanne als Chasselas kennenlernte, in seiner Markgrafschaft einführte und ihr diesen deutschen Namen gab. Der Gutedel, auch „Markgräfler" genannt, ist der typischste Wein des Markgräflerlandes. Er hat etwas Evangelisches an sich, ist klar, herb und etwas spritzig; genau der Wein, der am besten zu Speck und Rahmkäse passt. Er wächst überall, wo im Markgräfler Land Wein angebaut wird, wenn er nicht dem Riesling, dem Traminer und Gewürztraminer weichen muss.

Im badischen Oberland war es früher üblich, Neugeborene in Wein zu baden. Wohl wusste man damals schon um die desinfizierende Wirkung des Alkohols im Wein. Im 17. Jh. beschäftigte im badischen Unterland bei Karlsruhe eine Nottaufe mit Wein die Gemüter. Die Hebamme habe nicht lange nach Wasser gesucht, das im Brunnen zu holen gewesen wäre, sondern habe dem bereitstehenden Weinkrug noch vorhandenen Wein entnommen und damit die Nottaufe vollzogen. Die Hebamme war wohl eine Oberländerin, die es, wie später Johann Peter Hebel, in die Residenz verschlagen hat, und den heimischen Brauch ohne Bedenken auch hier ausübte.

Badnerland ist Hebelland. Kaum eine Landschaft ist mit einem Dichter so sehr verwoben wie Baden mit dem Kirchen- und Kalendermann, dem heiteren Poeten und großen alemannischen Erzähler Johann Peter Hebel, dem Menschenfreund aus dem Wiesental. Er ist der gute Geist dieses Landes. Das Alemannische ist schwer zu begreifen, der Schwarzwälder schwer zu verstehen. Doch darf man nicht den Fehler begehen, die Umständlichkeit des Sprechens mit der Umständlichkeit des Denkens zu verwechseln, wenn auch ein Schwarzwälder niemals ein Ich-liebe-dich über die Lippen bringen würde und man erst nach dem zweiten Viertele erahnt, dass er etwas für einen empfindet. Niemand hudelt in Baden.

Französische und österreichische Einflüsse wirken bis heute in der badischen Küche nach, wie sich auch der Austausch mit der Schweiz bemerkbar macht. Es ist ein Merkmal dieser Küche, dass sie soviel Freiheit lässt. Sie ist liberaler, weiter, offener als anderswo, genauso wie die Badener selbst das süße Nichtstun lieben und weitschweifiges Erzählen, das sich immer auf den tieferen Sinn des Lebens richtet, wie in den Geschichten Johann Peter Hebels.

Der geduldige Mann

Ein Mann, der eines Nachmittags müde nach Hause kam, hätte gern ein Stück Butterbrot mit Schnittlauch darauf gegessen, oder etwas von einem geräucherten Bug. Aber die Frau, die im Haus ziemlich der Meister war, und in der Küche ganz, hatte den Schlüssel zum Küchenkästlein in der Tasche, und war bei einer Freundin auf Besuch. Er schickte daher die Magd und den Knecht eins um das andere, die Frau soll heimkommen, oder den Schlüssel schicken. Sie sagte allemal: „Ich komm gleich, er soll nur ein wenig

> *At Müllen's Post Inn,*
> *To pass by would be a sin!*
> *A glass of good wine after toil*
> *Is something that will never spoil,*
> *At Müllen's Post Inn!*

JOHANN PETER HEBEL

Baden is where the Gutedel grows, also called "Markgräfler". There is something Evangelical about it. It is clear and dry and somewhat tangy; just the right wine to go with bacon and cream cheese. It grows wherever vines are cultivated, unless forced to give way to Riesling, Traminer or Gewürztraminer.

In Upper Baden, new-born children used to be bathed in wine. In those days the disinfectant effect of the alcohol in wine was probably already known. In the 17th century, an emergency baptism with wine in Lower Baden near Karlsruhe had the people there shaking their heads! The midwife, it is said, did not waste time looking for water, which she would have had to fetch from the well, but used the wine left in a handy wine jug to perform the ceremony! The midwife was probably from Upper Baden and, like Johann Peter Hebel after her, had gravitated to the royal seat, practising the customs of her homeland without reservations even in the capital.

Baden country is Hebel country. There is hardly a region so closely interwoven with a poet as Baden is with this churchman and calendar contributor, the cheerful poet and great Alemannic storyteller Johann Peter Hebel, the humanitarian from Wiesental. He is the good spirit of this country. Alemannic is a hard dialect to follow, and the inhabitants of the Black Forest are difficult to understand. But one should not make the mistake of confusing ponderousness of speech with complication of thinking, even if a Black Forester would never say anything as simple as I-love-you, and it is only after the second glass of wine that you vaguely realize that he feels some kind of emotion towards you. Nobody rushes things here in Baden.

French and Austrian influence can still be seen today in Baden's cuisine, and the close contacts with Switzerland are just as noticeable. One great feature of Baden cuisine is that it offers so much freedom. It is more liberal, broader-based, more open than elsewhere, just as the inhabitants of Baden themselves love the *dolce fa niente* and rambling tales always aimed at the deeper sense of life, like the stories of Johann Peter Hebel.

The patient man

A man who arrived home tired one afternoon would have liked to eat a slice of buttered bread with chives, or a piece of smoked shoulder of beef. But his wife, who was very much the master of the household and absolute mistress of the kitchen, had the key to the small kitchen cupboard in her bag and had gone to visit a friend. So he sent the maid and then the farmhand, one after the other, to tell his wife to either come home or send the key. She said to both: "I'll be right back, tell him to be a little patient." But as his patience wore thin and his hunger gnawed deeper, he and the farmhand carried the locked cupboard to the house of the friend his wife was visiting. He said to his wife: "Wife, be so good as to unlock me the cupboard so I can take something out for my supper, other-

warten." Als ihm aber die Geduld immer näher zusammenging und der Hunger immer weiter auseinander, trägt er und der Knecht das verschlossene Küchenkäschtlein in das Haus der Freundin, wo seine Frau zum Besuch war und sagt zu seiner Frau: „Frau, sei so gut und schließ mir das Kästlein auf, dass ich etwas zum Abendessen nehmen kann, sonst halt ich's nimmer aus." Also lachte die Frau und schnitt ihm ein Stücklein Brot herab und etwas vom Bug.

Da, wo früher Vorderösterreich war und die Wälder bedrohlich, stehen die Kirschwasserflasche und die Weihwasserflasche noch immer dicht beieinander. Da sucht man nach dem mütterlichen Schutz, da gibt es noch starke Frauenpersönlichkeiten, hat es viele Muttergottes-Wallfahrtsorte. Zudem beharren die Badener auf der Küche der Mütter. Deshalb gibt es hier auch soviele Rezepte für die Linzer Torte, wie es Familien gibt. Die Linzer Torte genießt man hierzulande mit einem Glas Gutedel, weil dieser den Geschmack der Nüsse hervorhebt.

In Baden hängt der Himmel voller köstlicher Speckseiten. Das war nicht immer so. Der Schwarzwald war lange Zeit Notstandsgebiet, was an der Erbregelung lag, nach der der Hof ungeteilt an den Jüngsten geht. Der Kartoffel ist es zu verdanken, dass ein Großteil der Bevölkerung im 18. Jh. nicht verhungerte. Sie bringt auch noch in Lagen, in denen kein Korn mehr gedieh, gute Erträge. Durch sie hatte man mehr Winternahrung und konnte die stille, schneereiche Zeit, die fast Dreiviertel des Jahres ausmachte, für den Nebenerwerb nutzen, der bald Haupterwerb werden sollte, die Uhrmacherei. Fünfzehn Millionen haben sie bis zur ersten Hälfte des 19. Jhs. hergestellt und verkauft. Sie sind in die Welt gezogen als Uhrenmacher und Uhrenhändler – bis nach Amerika, Russland und auf den Balkan – und erwarben neue Erkenntnisse. Wenn sie dann

nach Hause kamen, waren sie gemachte Männer und legten ihr Geld häufig in der Gastronomie an. Wirtshäuser im Schwarzwald heißen fast alle: Engel, Löwen, Ochsen, Adler. Sie wurden jeweils einem Evangelisten zugeordnet: Matthäus, Markus, Lukas und Johannes. Ohne diese Zentren der politischen Meinungsbildung und des Fabulierens wäre der Badener ein armer Kerli.

Nördlich des Breisgaus beginnt die Ortenau. Sie reicht bis Baden-Baden, das einstige Weltbad für blaublütige Gäste aus allen Höfen Europas und große Schriftsteller wie Dostojewski und Mark Twain. In Zeiten, in denen Paris die Winter-Metropole der eleganten Welt war, übernahm Baden-Baden mit seiner schönsten deutschen Spielbank diese Rolle den Sommer über. Badens sprachliche und kulturelle Grenze im Norden bildet die Murg.

Ganz im Süden des Schwarzwalds, dort, wo die Bäume nie in den Himmel gewachsen sind und Freiheitskämpfe tobten, schrieb Joseph Victor von Scheffel in einer der ehemals freien Waldstädte, die einst zur Voderösterreichischen Provinz gehörten, über die typische Seele der dortigen Bauernhäuser: „Eine Ofenbank, die man sonderbarerweise ‚Kunst' nennt, und die auch während der Winterszeit den Mittelpunkt der Tätigkeit manches Biedermanns bildet, indem er darauf den edlen und freien Künsten des Schnapstrinkens und Schlafens gleichmäßig obliegt." Und das Schnapsbrennen lag ihnen schon immer im Blut.

Wer einst eine Schwarzwälder Uhr gekauft hatte, konnte selbst in England damit rechnen, dass jedes Jahr ein Schwarzwälder vorbeikam, die Uhr reinigte, regulierte und im Bedarfsfall reparierte. Wenn der Badener etwas macht, dann macht er es eben recht. So hält er es auch mit dem Kochen. Wenn er kocht, dann öbbis Rechts!

wise I'll die of hunger!" His wife laughed and cut him a slice of bread and a piece of the smoked shoulder of beef.

In the region that was once Outer Austria, where the forests loom ominously, the bottle of cherry schnapps and the bottle of holy water are never far apart. This is where motherly protection is sought, this is where there are still strong female personalities, where there are many places of pilgrimage connected with the Blessed Virgin Mary. The Badeners stick to their mothers' cuisine. And she always preferred the red-spotted brook trout, even in times when there were still salmon in our streams and rivers. On Lake Constance, lake trout and perch, called "Kretzer" in Swabian and "Egli" in the Swiss dialect, are much appreciated. The best apples in the world are grown along Lake Constance, or so they say. Baden – a land of milk and honey.

In Baden, delicious sides of bacon did not always hang high.

For a long time the Black Forest was a distressed area due to the inheritance laws whereby the farm passed, undivided, to the youngest son. It is only thanks to the potato that a large proportion of the population of the Black Forest escaped starvation in the 18th century. It provided the population with more to eat in winter, and they could use the quiet, snow-bound months which accounted for almost three quarters of the year for a part-time occupation which soon became a major source of income: clock-making. Fifteen million had been made and sold by the first half of the 19th century. They travelled the world as clock-makers and clock-dealers. As far as America, Russia and the Balkans, always making new discoveries. When they returned home, they had made their fortunes and mainly invested their money in gastronomy.

Here in the Black Forest, great beers are brewed. Inns are rarely called anything but The Angel, The Lion, The Ox, The Eagle. Each named after one of the Evangelists: Matthew, Mark, Luke and John. Without his inns, those centres of political opinion-formation and story-telling, the Badener would be a poor chap indeed!

The Ortenau region begins north of Breisgau. It stretches as far as Baden-Baden, the erstwhile mundane spa for blue-blooded guests from every court in Europe and great authors. In times when Paris was the winter metropolis of the elegant world, Baden-Baden, with the most attractive casino in Germany, took over this role in summer. Baden's linguistic and cultural northern border is unavoidably marked by the River Murg.

In the very south, in one of the formerly free Forest Towns that once belonged to the province of Outer Austria, Joseph Victor von Scheffel wrote about the typical "soul" of the farmhouses there: there was, he said, a bench against the stove bearing the strange name "Kunst" (= art) and which, even during the winter months, formed the focus of the activity of many an honest citizen, who devoted himself to the noble and free "arts" of schnapps drinking and sleeping in equal measure.

Anyone who bought a Black Forest cuckoo clock in those days could, even in England, count on someone from the Black Forest calling once a year to clean and regulate the clock and, if needs be, even to repair it. When someone from Baden does or makes something, he does or makes it properly. And so it is with cooking. When he or she cooks, it is always "something proper"!